One Step at a Time, Intermediate 2

One Step at a Time, Intermediate 2

Judith D. García

Miami-Dade Community College
Kendall Campus

Heinle & Heinle Publishers
An International Thomson Publishing Company
Boston, Massachusetts, 02116, USA

Heinle & Heinle Publishers
20 Park Plaza
Boston, MA 02116 U.S.A.

International Thomson Publishing
Berkshire House 168–173
High Holborn
London WC1V7AA
England

Thomas Nelson Australia
102 Dodds Street
South Melbourne, 3205
Victoria, Australia

Nelson Canada
1120 Birchmont Road
Scarborough, Ontario
Canada M1K5G4

International Thomson
    Publishing Gmbh
Königwinterer Strasse 418
53227 Bonn
Germany

International Thomson
    Publishing Asia
Block 221 Henderson Road
    #08–03
Henderson Industrial Park
Singapore 0315

International Thomson
    Publishing—Japan
Hirakawacho-cho Kyowa
    Building, 3F
2-2-1 Hirakawacho-cho
Chiyoda-ku, 102 Tokyo
Japan

The publication of *One Step at a Time, Intermediate 2* was directed by the members of the Newbury House Publishing Team at Heinle & Heinle:

Erik Gundersen, Editorial Director
John F. McHugh, Market Development Director
Kristin Thalheimer, Production Services Coordinator
Maryellen Eschmann Killeen, Production Editor
Amy Lawler, Managing Development Editor

Also participating in the publication of this program:

Publisher: Stanley J. Galek
Director of Production: Elizabeth Holthaus
Project Manager: Hockett Editorial Service
Senior Assistant Editor: Ken Pratt
Manufacturing Coordinator: Mary Beth Hennebury
Interior Designer and Compositor: Greta D. Sibley
Cover Designer: Gina Petti•Rotunda Design
Photo/Video Specialist: Jonathan Stark
Illustrator: Robert Holmes

Photo credits (page numbers appear in bold): Jean-Claude LeJeune, Stock Boston—**1;** Harvey Lloyd, Stock Market—**21;** Peter Southwick, Stock Boston—**47;** C.J. Allen, Stock Boston—**125.**

Library of Congress Cataloging-in-Publication Data
Garcia, Judith.
        One step at a time.   Intermediate 2 / Judith D. Garcia.
          p.   cm.
        Summary : An introduction, intended for students who are not
    native English-speakers, to writing descriptive and process paragraphs.
        ISBN 0-8384-50318
        1. English language--Textbooks for foreign speakers.   [1. English
    language--Textbooks for foreign speakers.   2. English language-
    -Paragraphs.] I. Title.
        PE1128.G25   1995
    428.2'4--dc20   95-46028
                                                                                          CIP
                                                                                          AC

Heinle & Heinle Publishers is a division of International Thomson Publishing, Inc.

Manufactured in the United States of America.

ISBN 0-8384-50318

10 9 8 7 6 5 4 3 2 1

Contents

CHAPTER 3
Paragraphs of Comparison **47**

CHAPTER 4
Paragraphs of Contrast **73**

CHAPTER 4 SUPPLEMENT

CHAPTER 5

CHAPTER 5 SUPPLEMENT

Preface

One Step at a Time, Intermediate 2 is the second of a two-level academic writing series for learners of English. It is an intermediate writing text with accompanying skill-developing, interactive computer software programs for both the Windows and Macintosh platforms.

The complete *One Step at a Time* program has been developed to meet the needs of writing students at the low intermediate and intermediate levels and includes the following components:

- *One Step at a Time, Intermediate 1*
  - Text
  - Computerized interactive tutorials
    - Individual Macintosh package
    - Institutional Macintosh package
    - Macintosh demo
    - Individual Windows package
    - Institutional Windows package
    - Windows demo

- *One Step at a Time, Intermediate 2*
  - Text
  - Computerized interactive tutorials
    - Individual Macintosh package
    - Institutional Macintosh package
    - Macintosh demo
    - Individual Windows package
    - Institutional Windows package
    - Windows demo

The text is designed for a forty-hour course. It consists of six chapters which take approximately four hours of classroom work each. Each of the six chapters also has an optional supplement which can take one or two hours. The computerized interactive tutorials are thoroughly cross-referenced with the text and provide hours of additional practice.

OBJECTIVES OF ONE STEP AT A TIME, *INTERMEDIATE 2*

By the end of the course, the student will:

Plan and develop a paragraph with a topic sentence, body (containing major and secondary supports) and conclusion.
   a. Use appropriate paragraph form.
   b. Use logical organization.
   c. Write with clarity and coherence.
   d. Use language appropriate to audience and purpose.

Write expository paragraphs using the following:
   a. Illustration and example.
   b. Classification.
   c. Comparison/contrast.
   d. Definition.

Write a variety of simple, compound and complex sentences.
   a. Use parts of speech correctly.
   b. Use appropriate capitalization, punctuation, and spelling.
   c. Use correct word order.
   d. Use appropriate transition words.
   e. Edit sentences and paragraphs.

As with Book 1 of the One Step series, the chapters of this text do not adhere to a rigid structure, and may include from two to four sections depending on the content and objectives of the chapter. Each chapter guides the student through the basic grammatical structures and sentence patterns needed to create academic paragraphs of illustration, comparison, contrast, classification, and definition. The chapters include the basic grammatical structures, sentence patterns, and punctuation required to develop these academic paragraphs. Students are guided through the process of developing topic sentences appropriate to the rhetorical focus of each paragraph; planning the support for the topic sentence (brainstorming, listing, clustering, outlining); writing a variety of sentence patterns for the primary and secondary supporting details; and developing good conclusions. The grammatical structures and sentence patterns that students need to use to write each type of paragraph are introduced in each chapter. Additional exercises and explanations of the principal patterns are offered in chapter supplements at the end of the book.

Each chapter contains various individual and collaborative writing tasks which help students practice and internalize the writing, punctuation, and grammar concepts presented in the lessons.

The editing symbols section at the end of each chapter teaches students to recognize and correct from three to six common writing errors. For each of these sections, there is a computer program, which takes from one to two hours to complete. There is also a "personal vocabulary builder" program for the Macintosh that will allow students to create their own interactive dictionaries as they learn English. They can add new words to their computer dictionary, take a test, review missed words, and print their scores.

All of the software programs for this text are relevant to, but not repetitive of the text exercises. In some of the software programs, there are collaborative learning activities. At the end of each computer program, the students can print a test covering the concepts taught in the software program.

OBJECTIVES OF ONE STEP AT A TIME, *INTERMEDIATE 1*

By the end of the course, the student will:

Plan and develop a paragraph with a topic sentence, body (containing major supports), and conclusion.
   a. Use appropriate paragraph form.
   b. Use logical organization.
   c. Write with clarity and coherence.

Write narrative and descriptive paragraphs using the following:
   a. Chronological sequence (process).
   b. Spatial sequence (in descriptions).

Write a variety of simple, compound, and complex sentences using coordinating conjunctions, subordinating conjunctions, and transitional words and expressions.
   a. Use parts of speech correctly.
   b. Use appropriate capitalization, punctuation, and spelling.
   c. Use correct word order.
   d. Edit sentences and paragraphs.

COMPUTERIZED INTERACTIVE TUTORIALS

Computerized interactive tutorials are provided as a supplement to the text's grammar objectives (present and present continuous tenses, adverbs of frequency, parts of speech and sentence building, sentence connecting, pronouns and possessive adjectives, adjectives in noun clauses). Interactive computer exercises are also provided to give students practice with such paragraph development skills as focusing topics, developing controlling ideas, and writing topic sentences. The computerized tutorials are thoroughly cross-referenced with the text; the computer disk logo indicates ideal times at which teachers and students might use the software.

Introduction to
Academic Writing

The computer programs that accompany this chapter are called: **Chapter 1— Disk 1A** and **"Personal Vocabulary Builder"—Disk 1B**

Discuss the following questions with a partner, in a small group, or as a class.

1. What is academic writing?

2. How is academic writing different from other writing?

3. What is a paragraph?

AUTHOR, AUDIENCE, AND PURPOSE

All writing has three things in common: an author who writes, that author's purpose for writing, and the audience who will read the writing. Let's look at each of these elements.

Author: The most important factor in any writing is you, the **author.** You are unique, and when you write, you show a personal side of yourself to your reader. As you express your ideas, personal experiences, special interests, attitudes, feelings, fears, or hopes in your writing, your reader will see special aspects of your personality, how you think, and how well you write. This is why it is important to learn to express yourself well in writing.

Audience: All writing has an **audience,** somebody who reads your writing. Sometimes that audience is you (the author). When you are your own audience, writing style is very flexible. For example, the study notes you take in your classes or the list you make before you go to the grocery store are for your own personal information, and nobody else will read them. For this kind of writing, you do not need to pay attention to grammar, spelling, or punctuation because you understand your **meaning.**

However, your audience is usually somebody else, and you must think about that audience when you write. Sometimes you have to change your writing style to make sure your audience can understand and appreciate your ideas. This means that you have to know your audience before you write.

To understand how a particular audience can change the way you write, think of a typical grocery list. A list that you write for yourself is very different from a list you would write for your young daughter or for your roommate. When you are your own audience, you will understand your own messy handwriting and abbreviations such as

2 tom

OJ

t.p.

brd

However, for your daughter or roommate, you would probably write:

> 2 large red tomatoes (not too soft)
>
> 1 gallon orange juice
>
> 1 4-pack of toilet paper
>
> 1 loaf Publix brown bread

The audience you have in mind will influence the language style you use. The audience for academic writing in an ESL writing class is probably your teacher or classmate. The language you will use in that class is Standard American English (SAE). You will not use slang expressions, informal words, or words that belong to a special (nonstandard) dialect of American English.

Purpose: The third important characteristic of academic writing is the **purpose**—the reason for writing. People write for one of three reasons: to inform, to entertain, or to persuade. Academic writing textbooks usually teach students to write paragraphs or compositions that narrate, describe, define, illustrate, classify, compare/contrast, analyze, or persuade. There is always a purpose for writing, and your purpose will influence your writing in many ways. The vocabulary you use, the length of your sentences, and even your handwriting will change, depending upon your audience and your purpose.

Exercise 1.1 The author, audience, and purpose of each paragraph in the following two sets of paragraphs are different. With a classmate, determine the author, audience, and purpose for each paragraph. Discuss how the writing style and tone change from paragraph to paragraph.

1A.

The purpose of this memorandum is to inform you that, due to circumstances beyond my control, I must resign my position as coach of the softball team as of the 15th of this month. Please send my severance check to the following address: ...

Author: _____

Audience: _____

Purpose: _____

Describe the writing style and tone in this paragraph. Is it serious? Informal? Formal? Funny?

1B.

First, let me say that coaching this team has been a real pleasure, and I'm sure you'll be the state champions this year. I am sorry to say I won't be here to see that happen since my family and I will be moving to California in a couple of weeks. I have enjoyed being your coach and will miss you all. Please let me know how you do in the state finals. My address in California will be...

Author: _____

Audience: _____

Purpose: _____

Describe the writing style and tone in this paragraph.

1C.

Sweetheart! Guess what??? I got the job in California. We leave in two weeks!!! Let's celebrate tonight—pick any restaurant you like. (Why don't you wear the blue suit and the gray tie I got you for Father's Day?) Love ya!

Author: _____

Audience: _____

Purpose: _____

Describe the writing style and tone in this paragraph. Is the author a man or a woman?

2A.

Dear Professor Mitchell:

I will not be able to attend class tomorrow because I must go to a funeral. If possible, could you please give any handouts to my friend Jorge Contreras? I will be in class again on Monday. Thank you for your understanding....

John Smith

Author: _____

Audience: _____

Purpose: _____

Describe the writing style and tone in this paragraph.

2B.

Mark—I'm cutting class tomorrow. Going to the Crandon Park beach. Maria and Susana are going too, it'll be a blast! Come with us. Meet us in the student parking lot #3 at 9:00—Bring the soda—we got the chips and the music. Yo—Don't tell Jorge about the beach—I want him to pick up the homework in class for me.

John

Author: _____

Audience: _____

Purpose: _____

Describe the writing style and tone in this paragraph. Is the paragraph grammatically correct?

2C.

Jorge: I won't be in class tomorrow. Could you do me a favor and pick up any handouts that the teacher gives in class? I'll go by your house tomorrow to get them from you. (Also, if Professor Mitchell asks, tell her my aunt died.) Thanks,

John

Author: _____

Audience: _____

Purpose: _____

Describe the writing style and tone in this paragraph.

2D.

To: Dr. Dominguez, Chair of International Students Program
From: Professor Mitchell
Re: Absence from work tomorrow

This is to inform you that I will not be on campus tomorrow. I have arranged for a substitute to cover my classes. Please count my absence as a personal leave day. I will be chaperoning my daughter's Environmental Club to Crandon Park Beach.

Author: _____

Audience: _____

Purpose: _____

Describe the writing style and tone in this paragraph. Do you think John is going to have an unpleasant surprise at the beach tomorrow?

Exercise 1.2 Write for five minutes. The topic is: "The importance of author, audience, and purpose in academic writing." Use your own paper for this exercise.

Exercise 1.3 Sit with a partner for this exercise. Rewrite the following sentences so that the language and tone fit the new audience.

1. This is a note for a husband or wife. Rewrite this message for a ten-year-old child:

   Honey, please pick up chicken, milk, lettuce, and apples on your way home today.

   _____

   _____

   _____

2. This is a note for a friend. Rewrite this message for the teacher:

   I have to cut writing class today—gotta study for a history exam. Please tell the prof I'm sick—I'll get the homework from you tonight. Later! and Thanks!

   John

   _____

   _____

   _____

3. This is part of a conversation between two friends. Rewrite this same idea as though you were expressing the opinion in a speech in front of the class at school.

   "Man! It really bugs me when people treat others rotten just 'cause they're a different color or religion. It's just plain stupid!"

   _____

   _____

   _____

INTRODUCTION TO ACADEMIC PARAGRAPHS

What is a paragraph? A paragraph looks like this:

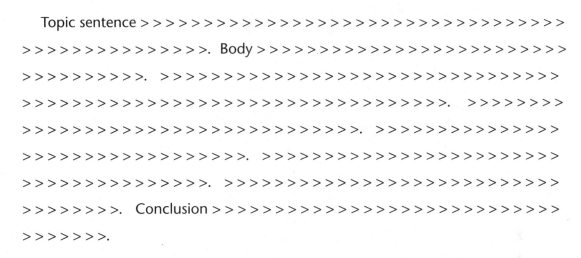

The first line of the paragraph is indented five spaces. The left margin of the paragraph is even, but the right margin is not. If a sentence ends in the middle of a line on the paper, the next sentence follows immediately after it—not on the next line. Many teachers prefer double-spaced paragraphs because it gives them an area to write comments and corrections. As you write your paragraphs, use the following checklist to see if you have used the correct paragraph format:

Paragraph Format Checklist

__ 1. I indented the first line.

__ 2. I double-spaced (skipped lines).

__ 3. I did not start each sentence on a new line.

__ 4. I capitalized the first letter of each sentence.

__ 5. I used at least five periods in the paragraph.

What is an *academic* paragraph? An academic paragraph is a group of sentences with a topic sentence, a body, and a conclusion. The number of sentences in an academic paragraph varies according to the type of paragraph you are writing. In an intermediate ESL class, most paragraphs are at least five to eight sentences long, and they are written in Standard American English (see above). Each paragraph develops one (and **only one**) idea.

Exercise 1.4 Discuss the format of these paragraphs with a partner: What is wrong with each one?

1.

_____
_____. _____
_____
_____. _____
_____
_____
_____.

Problem: _____

2.

_____
_____. _____
_____. _____
_____. _____
_____
_____. _____
_____.

Problem: _____

3.

_____
_____
_____.
_____. _____
_____.
_____.

Problem: _____

The Topic Sentence

The first sentence of an academic paragraph is usually the **topic sentence.** It tells the reader what you are going to write about (the **focused topic**) and what you are going to say about that topic (the **controlling idea**).

Example

Of all the history professors at this college, **Professor James** is the most **creative.**

Focused topic: Professor James

Controlling idea: creative

The topic in your topic sentence must be limited (focused) because it must be completely developed in one paragraph. Your controlling idea in the topic sentence must be interesting to both you and your audience. In advanced academic writing classes, your paragraphs will have topic sentences in the middle or at the end, but for now, your topic sentence should be the first sentence of every paragraph you write.

• Topic Sentence Don't's[1]

There are only three "Do's" to remember when you write a topic sentence:

1. Focus the topic.

2. Choose an excellent controlling idea.

3. Write the focused topic and the controlling idea in one complete sentence.

It sounds easy, doesn't it? But students have ten common problems when they are learning to develop topic sentences. The following "Don't's" are rules you can use to check your topic sentence **before** you begin to develop your paragraph. The rules are explained in detail with examples and exercises in the Chapter 1 Supplement on page 147.

About the topic sentence in general:

Don't #1	Don't write a fragment as a topic sentence.
Don't #2	Don't announce the topic (no "This paragraph will discuss...").
Don't #3	Don't state the topic sentence as a personal opinion (no "I believe that..." or "I think that...").
Don't #4	Don't include the paragraph's supporting ideas in the topic sentence.

About the focused topic:

Don't #5	Don't forget to focus the topic.
Don't #6	Don't write more than one focused topic in the topic sentence.
Don't #7	Don't omit the topic.

---

1 The idiomatic expression "the do's and don'ts" refers to any set of rules or advice to explain how to do and NOT to do something.

About the controlling idea:

Don't #8   Don't omit the controlling idea.

Don't #9   Don't write more than one controlling idea.

Don't #10   Don't use vague words as controlling ideas.

As you write your topic sentence, make sure you check it for the following:

Topic Sentence Checklist

___ 1. I have only one topic, and I have focused my topic.

___ 2. I have one (and only one) excellent controlling idea.

___ 3. My topic sentence is complete.

Exercise 1.5—Topic Sentences Discuss the errors in the following topic sentences with a partner. The number in the right column refers to the "topic sentence Don't." Write each topic sentence correctly. Refer to the list of *Topic Sentence Don't's* in the Supplement at the end of this chapter to find an explanation of each error.

Sentences with Errors	Topic Sentence Don't
1. How to bake potatoes in a microwave oven.	#1
2. The television is not on.	#8
3. Harvey is generous with his friends and handsome.	#9
4. He is the most creative teacher at this school.	#7
5. I believe that drugs should never be legalized in the United States.	#3
6. Government is corrupt.	#5
7. John has an eccentric lifestyle because he is a millionaire and travels to a different country every day, and while he is in each country, he goes to nightclubs and volunteers to play the piano for free.	#4
8. The topic of this paragraph will be foreign import cars.	#2
9. The computer and the telephone were important inventions this century.	#6
10. Dogs are nice.	#10

The Body

The **body** of your paragraph must contain supporting ideas (usually three) that develop the topic sentence. You develop each supporting idea with one or two additional sentences that give details, examples, or explanation. The organization of these ideas depends on your purpose for the paragraph. For example, if your paragraph describes a process, you will put the steps of the process in chronological order so your reader can understand it, but in a persuasive paragraph you will present your ideas with the most important point either first or last.

The important thing to remember is that all of the ideas in the body of your paragraph must develop the controlling idea in your topic sentence. Before you turn in any paragraph, use the checklist below to see that you have all of the essential details and that they all relate to the topic sentence.

The Body of the Paragraph (Checklist)

___ 1. I have at least three supporting ideas.

___ 2. Each of my supports is explained with secondary support (details, examples, facts, etc.).

___ 3. Each of my supporting ideas develops the controlling idea.

Exercise 1.6—Supporting Sentences What is wrong with the supporting sentences in these paragraphs? Underline the sentences that are not correct, and then explain the problem.

1.

Of all the people who live on our block, Peter White looks the meanest. He has a hard little mouth with pale thin lips that never smile. He lives in San Francisco with his mother and sister. They do not like him very much. The expression in his eyes is usually cold and cruel. When you look at Peter, you wonder if his face could possibly be a reflection of his personality.

Problem: _____

2.

Princess Diana and Mother Teresa are similar in several ways. Both women are famous people, and both are charismatic and popular with the mighty as well as the humble. Mother Teresa is much older than Princess Diana, and Princess Diana is surrounded by power, political intrigue, and public scrutiny. Both Princess Diana and Mother Teresa care for the poor and the ill. I greatly admire both women for the qualities they have in common.

Problem: _____

3.

It can be advantageous to have a small family in the United States rather than a large one. First of all, in small families, less money is needed for the basic necessities of the family members, so there is often more money available for better food, education, health care, and leisure activities. This is why having a small family in the United States is better than having a large one.

Problem: _____

The Conclusion

The **conclusion** of your paragraph finishes the development of your controlling idea. It can contain your opinion, advice, an invitation to your reader, a restatement (but in different words) of your topic sentence, or a summary of the main points of the paragraph. Just like the body, your conclusion must relate directly to your topic sentence. It should name your focused topic again but not simply repeat your topic sentence. The checklist below will help you check the conclusions of your paragraphs.

The Conclusion (Checklist)

__ 1. My conclusion names the focused topic again.

__ 2. My conclusion finishes the development of my controlling idea.

__ 3. My conclusion gives an invitation, a restatement (but in different words) of the topic sentence, advice, an opinion, or a summary of the topic sentence.

Exercise 1.7—Concluding Sentences What is wrong with the conclusion of each of the paragraphs below?

1.

The Labrador retriever is a wonderful house pet for families. Most Labs have a very gentle and tolerant nature, and they are patient dogs. This makes them wonderful pets for even the youngest children of a family. Furthermore, the Labs are famous for their intelligence. They can easily be trained to do tricks and to fetch papers, shoes, and slippers. This be entertaining for the whole family. Yet another special quality of Labs is their size. Because they are large dogs, and their size may serve to intimidate burglars or prowlers from entering a family's home, they are perfect guardians for homes. **The Labrador retriever is a wonderful house pet for families.**

Problem: _____

2.

The Labrador retriever is a wonderful house pet for families. Most Labs have a very gentle and tolerant nature, and they are patient dogs. This makes them wonderful pets for even the youngest children of a family. Furthermore, the Labs are famous for their intelligence. They can easily be trained to do tricks and to fetch papers, shoes, and slippers. This can be entertaining for the whole family. Yet another special quality of Labs is their size. Because they are large dogs, and their size may serve to intimidate burglars or prowlers from entering a family's home, they are perfect guardians for homes. **Cats also make good house pets.**

Problem: _____

3.

The Labrador retriever is a wonderful house pet for families. Most Labs have a very gentle and tolerant nature, and they are patient dogs. This makes them wonderful pets for even the youngest children of a family. Furthermore, the Labs are famous for their intelligence. They can easily be trained to do tricks and to fetch papers, shoes, and slippers. This can be entertaining for the whole family. Yet another special quality of Labs is their size. Because they are large dogs, and their size may serve to intimidate burglars or prowlers from entering a family's home, they are perfect guardians for homes. **Not everyone likes the Lab.**

Problem: _____

Exercise 1.8 Rewrite each of the three paragraphs from Exercise 1.6 on your own paper. Make sure that each paragraph has three supporting ideas that develop the topic sentence. **For the second paragraph, select either Princess Diana OR Mother Teresa—not both.** Name each paragraph as follows:

Paragraph #1: "Peter White"

Paragraph #2: "Mother Teresa" (or "Princess Diana")

Paragraph #3: "Advantages of Having a Small Family"

When your teacher returns these paragraphs to you, do not throw them away. You will use them for later exercises in the book.

Exercise 1.9—Self-Check Answer the following questions in complete sentences. Pay attention to punctuation and grammar in your responses.

1. What do "author," "audience," and "purpose" mean?

   _____

2. What are the three parts of an academic paragraph?

   _____

3. What is a focused topic?

   _____

4. What is a controlling idea?

   _____

5. Why is a controlling idea important in a paragraph?

   _____

6. What can you write in a conclusion to a paragraph?

   _____

7. What does an academic paragraph look like?

   _____

EDITING SYMBOLS

Introduction

Different teachers use different methods of correcting writing papers. Some indicate errors by underlining words or parts of sentences, and let the students correct the errors. Others correct every mistake on a writing assignment. Some teachers have students correct each other's work in class. Others don't correct writing errors at all.

A correction technique found in many academic writing books involves the use of editing symbols. These are standard symbols that teachers write on your paper to indicate what kind of error you have made in a word, sentence, or section of a paragraph. You use a reference list of symbols to see what kind of error you have made and how to correct it. These are the symbols that will be presented in this textbook. If your teacher doesn't use these editing symbols, don't worry. The purpose of this section is not to focus on the symbol, but rather on the error that it represents. In each chapter, a few of the most common writing errors will be explained in detail, with exercises to help you learn to correct them.

In the Chapter 1 Supplement (page 155), you will find a reference list for the editing symbols, with explanations and examples, and a checklist that you can use to keep track of your own writing errors.

Problems with Paragraph Form

Symbol	Meaning	Explanation
¶	New paragraph	Start a new paragraph (indent).
¶ OR **no** ¶	No new paragraph	Do NOT start a new paragraph here.

These symbols indicate that you have a problem with the structure of your paragraph. You forgot to indent the first line of your paragraph, you mistakenly divided the paragraph into two sections, or you wrote your paragraph as a list of sentences instead of as a paragraph.

Examples

The following four paragraphs should be written as only ONE paragraph, and the first line of the first paragraph needs to be indented. The second paragraph should not be a separate paragraph because it continues developing the anecdote. The last two lines should be part of the paragraph, too. The author began each one at the left margin, and they look like part of a list—not like part of the paragraph.

¶ There are important differences between a good student and a bad student. One of the differences is their behavior. For example, a good student, who always comes to class on time, is polite and kind, and always pays attention in class, while a bad student, who usually comes late, is rude and always seems distracted.

¶ Another difference is their study method. Whereas a good student studies hard and gets good grades, a bad student, who seldom does the homework and never studies seriously, gets low grades.

¶ Furthermore, a good student has a special personality which is serious and open-minded; in contrast, a bad student is irresponsible and stubborn.

¶ Now think about yourself and give a sincere answer: Which type of student are you?

Exercise 1.10 Rewrite the above paragraph using correct paragraph format. You can change any of the details of the paragraph that you want. Use the checklist on page 7 to check your work.

Problems with Topic Sentences *(foc, ci, off topic)*

● Focus *(foc)*

Symbol	Meaning	Explanation
foc	Focus	The topic is not focused. It is too general for one paragraph.

Examples:

> **Wrong:** **People** need to learn the language of that country quickly.
> *foc*

> **Correction:** **Immigrants** need to learn the language of their new country quickly.

> **Wrong:** **Crime** is dangerous for **people.**
> *foc*

> **Correction:** **Shoplifting** creates problems for **all consumers.**

The topic you select for your paragraph must not be too general. The topic must be focused enough to be completely developed with three ideas. If your topic is too general, the paragraph will be boring. To focus a topic, try to think of a subcategory or example of the topic like this:

> people
>
> people in America
>
> famous women in America
>
> famous female scientists in America
>
> famous female Nobel Prize winners in America
>
> Rosalyn Sussman Yalow

This listing technique can help you think about and then choose a focused topic. The form is not strict. For example, it is not necessary to repeat all of the words in every line. It is understood that each topic is a more specific example of the one above it:

> people
>
> Americans . . . .("who are people" is understood)
>
> famous women . . . .("who are American people" is understood)
>
> scientists . . . .("who are famous American women" is understood)
>
> Nobel Prize winners . . . .("who are famous American woman scientists" is understood)
>
> Rosalyn Sussman Yalow . .("a famous American woman scientist who won the Nobel Prize" is understood)

As you focus your topic, keep in mind that you are deciding on the topic for your paragraph. Your final focused topic needs to be one that interests you and will interest your audience. Maybe you do not know anything about the topic you wrote on the last line, and you are not interested enough to go to the library and research it. In that case, you have to focus the topic again.

More Examples

education	animals	technology
Venezuelan	domestic animals	computers
higher education	farm animals	IBM
pedagogical universities	poultry	word processing on the IBM
La Universidad Pedagógica de Barquisimeto	chickens	saving work to a floppy disk

How do you know when your topic is focused enough for one paragraph? Look at the **last line** of your list, and ask yourself the following questions.

Can I think of something interesting I want to say about this topic?

Will the topic interest my audience?

Do I have enough vocabulary to write a paragraph about this topic?

If the answers to your questions are "yes," then your topic is well focused and you are ready to find a controlling idea. If not, start the focusing process again.

Exercise 1.12 Focus these topics. Make sure that the focused topics interest you.

1. education   2. animals   3. technology   4. people   5. government

● Controlling idea (*ci*)

Symbol	Meaning	Explanation
ci	Controlling idea	The controlling idea is weak, missing, or not developed in the paragraph.

Example

Wrong: Jorge Luis Borges is a **nice** author.
                                    ci

Correction: Jorge Luis Borges is the **most famous** author in Argentina.

The topic sentence must contain a **controlling idea,** which is what you are going to say about your focused topic in the body of the paragraph. Since the controlling idea is going to be developed with three or more ideas, it must not be boring, vague, too specific, or missing. To find a controlling idea, you can use the techniques of brainstorming and concept mapping. Write the focused topic in the the middle of a piece of paper and draw a box around it.

chickens

Then think of everything that you could possibly say about your focused topic, and write them around the focused topic. If you want, you can write each idea in a bubble and connect it to the focused topic with a line. It is important to write every idea you think of, even if it sounds wrong to you. Later you will select just one of the ideas for your controlling idea, and you will ignore the weak ideas. Sometimes writers are afraid to write an idea on paper because they think it is not good. Then they hesitate and lose their train of thought. This brainstorming technique will help you find a controlling idea quickly IF you do **not** stop and tell yourself, "No, that's a dumb idea." Your concept map might look like this:

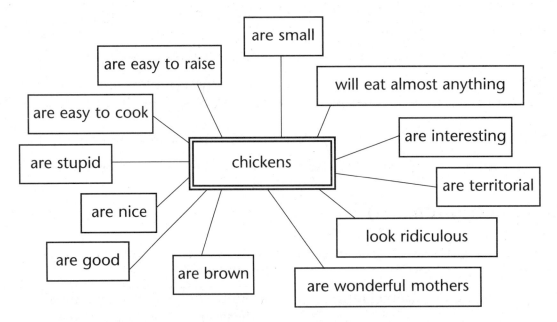

Now your job is to eliminate the bad controlling ideas. A bad controlling idea would be one that is vague, such as *good, bad, nice, interesting, big, little,* or *white.* These words are either too general *(good, bad, nice, interesting)* or too specific *(big, little, white),* and you should not write them in your topic sentence. Use the most precise and descriptive word you can find, one that will require at least three different supporting ideas to explain completely.

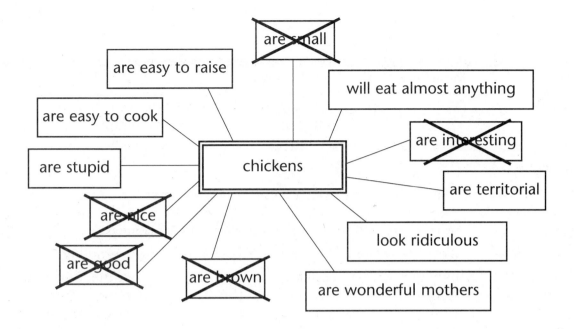

Now you have several good controlling ideas to choose from. Select the one you like the most. At this point, you need to ask yourself the following questions.

Is this controlling idea really true?

Can I think of three supporting ideas that prove this point about my topic?

Will my reader be interested in my paragraph if I choose this controlling idea?

If the answers to these questions are "yes," then you have a good controlling idea and are ready to plan the support of your topic sentence.

Exercise 1.12 Take the five focused topics (the **last** lines) from Exercise 1.9 on focusing topics, and on a separate piece of paper develop a concept map for each topic. Follow the process explained, and select a good controlling idea.

Now write topic sentences using the controlling ideas and focused topics from above.

1. _____

2. _____

3. _____

4. _____

5. _____

● Off topic

Symbol	Meaning	Explanation
off topic	Off topic	The topic of the topic sentence is not the same as the topic of the paragraph.

Example

Wrong: …**My father** has a wonderful smile. **My mother** has a nice personality….
off topic

THIS PARAGRAPH JUMPS FROM ONE TOPIC (FATHER) TO ANOTHER (MOTHER).

Correction: Write the paragraph about ONLY your father OR your mother.

This correction symbol means that the paragraph does not talk about the topic you introduced in the topic sentence. The topic sentence tells the reader what your paragraph will be about. If you tell your reader that you are going to write about chickens, and then in your paragraph you start comparing the chicken to a turkey, your paragraph is "off topic." If you want to compare turkeys and chickens, you must introduce both topics in the topic sentence.

Exercise 1.13 Read the following paragraphs with a partner. Underline the sentences in each paragraph that are "off topic."

Even though the Cold War is over, there remain in the world several famous intelligence agencies which still operate nationally and internationally. In Russia, for example, the KGB, or Committee of State Security, as well as the GRU, or Central Intelligence Office for Soviet military intelligence, still have a full-time staff and carry out special tasks and projects in Russia and abroad. Great Britain also operates both national and international Intelligence Agencies. The British Secret Intelligence Service is called MI-6, and the Defense Intelligence Staff for military intelligence is the DIA. Yet another country with a major intelligence service is France, with the SDECE (Service de Documentation Extérieure et de Contre-Espionnage) serving as both a national and an international agency for information and counterespionage. Being a spy in this day and age can be difficult. It takes a lot of training and education. Many spies must study for years to perfect foreign language skills. They travel all around the world on secret missions.

Charles is similar to Daren in three important ways. They share the same cultural background. Both grew up and were educated in Cuba. My own grandmother was also from Cuba, but not from the same city as Charles and Daren. Charles and Daren also share the same religious background. They are Catholics. I am Catholic, too, and sometimes I see them in church on Sundays. One last interesting similarity between Charles and Daren is that both share the same hobby. They love to fish. Key West is excellent for marlin fishing. As you can see, these two gentlemen share many interesting similarities.

chapter
two

Illustration
Through Examples

The computer programs that accompany the editing symbols in this chapter are called: **Chapter 2—Disk 1** and **"Personal Vocabulary Builder"—Disk 1B**

INTRODUCTION AND MODEL PARAGRAPHS

CLASSROOM ETIQUETTE

As immigrants or visiting students in the United States, it is important for you to learn about the cultural etiquette of your new country. What is acceptable behavior in some cultures may not be acceptable in others. In United States schools, for example, there are **rules of etiquette** that might be different from those in the schools of other countries. For instance, paying attention in class, arriving on time, and handing in neatly prepared homework are ways to show respect for teachers. Respect is shown to classmates by not interrupting others when they are speaking in class and by not laughing at their mistakes or accents. In the United States, it is not acceptable behavior for a student to leave the classroom in the middle of a class without asking permission, nor is it acceptable to interrupt the teacher when he or she is presenting information to the class as a group. Students who want to ask questions usually raise their hand and wait for the teacher to call on them. During examinations, seeking help from another student or from notes is not only rude behavior in the United States, it is the most frequent reason for student expulsion from colleges and universities. Students from foreign countries are sometimes shocked at this intolerance to cheating that exists in American schools. This is why it is important to understand not only the accepted behavior in U.S. schools, but also the dangerous consequences of not conforming to the accepted behavior.

Think and discuss:

1. Is **classroom etiquette** different in your country? What are the consequences of cheating in your country's schools?

2. Are there some topics that would not be good for a paragraph that uses examples? For example, would it be easier for you to give examples of important rivers in South America or examples of the Amazon river? Why?

3. What makes a good topic for a paragraph of examples?

4. With a partner, list five possible topics for a paragraph of examples.

Example:

Tourist attractions in this city

a. _____

b. _____

c. _____

d. _____

e. _____

You can use examples in the support of many different kinds of paragraphs (definition, comparison, contrast, process, description, and cause and effect). In this chapter, you will learn to develop the entire body of a paragraph using examples. The paragraph that uses examples gives several concrete details that explain a general concept. The body uses examples to explain the topic sentence, but it does not list or name all possible examples. The paragraph on the previous page, for example, uses several examples to explain "cultural etiquette in U.S. schools," but there are probably many more examples that you could think of for that topic.

It is often possible to organize the things you are explaining or describing into three or more categories, such as types, locations, varieties, or kinds. Classifying can help you organize the body of the paragraph logically, and it will help your reader follow your ideas. Notice that the details in the following two paragraphs are categorized into geographic locations of the fruit. The secondary support in the third paragraph below is improved with **adjective clauses,** which you can study on page 34 of this chapter and in the Chapter 2 Supplement on page 161.

Read the following three paragraphs with a partner, and answer the questions that follow them.

Many tropical fruits which are popular in their own country are not exported in great quantities, so most people in other countries are not familiar with them. These tropical fruits include the sapodilla, the mamoncillo, and the tuna. In addition, some people eat durian and mangosteen. Others enjoy the fruit of the passionflower. Although all of these tropical fruits are quite popular locally, they are not exported in great quantities, so most people in other countries are not familiar with them.

Many tropical fruits which are popular in their own country are not exported in great quantities, so most people in other countries are not familiar with them. Tropical fruits that are native to Central and South America, for example, include the sapodilla, the mamoncillo, and the tuna. In the East Indian islands, people eat durian and mangosteen. People who live in Australia enjoy the fruit of the passionflower. Although all of these tropical fruits are quite popular locally, they are not exported in great quantities, so most people **who** live in other countries are not familiar with them.

Many tropical fruits **which** are popular in their own country are not exported in great quantities, so most people in the other countries are not familiar with them. Tropical fruits **that** are native to Central and South America, for example, include the sapodilla, **which** tastes like pears and molasses; the mamoncillo, **which** is small, round, and bitter-sweet; and the tuna, a juicy fruit which grows on the nopal cactus. In the East Indian islands, people eat durian, a smelly but delicious fruit, and mangosteen, **which** tastes like a peach and a pineapple at the same time. People **who** live in Australia enjoy the fruit of the passionflower, **which** they call grenadilla, with cream or in salads. Although all of these tropical fruits are quite popular locally, they are not exported in great quantities, so most people **who** live in other countries are not familiar with them.

Exercise 2.1 Answer these questions about the paragraphs above.

1. How is the second paragraph different from the first? Which of the first two paragraphs sounds more complete? Why?

   _____

2. What has been added to the third paragraph? How do the details change the paragraph?

   _____

3. What is the topic of the paragraphs?

   _____

4. In paragraphs two and three, how are the three main supporting ideas divided in the paragraphs? List the three divisions here:

   a. _____

   b. _____

   c. _____

5. Look again at the above paragraphs and add the **examples** in the body of the paragraphs to the concept map below. Notice that the examples are divided into categories: geographical locations. This is a good technique for organizing the support in some paragraphs of examples.

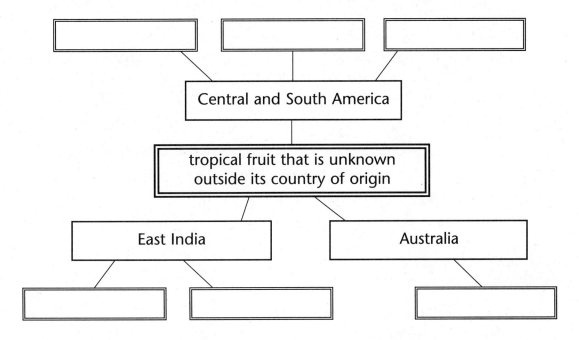

6. The conclusion to the paragraphs on tropical fruit is very weak. It only restates the topic sentences. Write a better conclusion for the paragraph (an invitation, some advice, or a suggestion).

_____

7. The **boldface** words in the last paragraph on the previous page are called relative pronouns. They introduce adjective clauses. Read the explanation of adjective clauses in the Chapter 2 Supplement (page 161).

THE TOPIC SENTENCE

Remember that in your paragraph of examples, you will use details to explain the topic sentence. You must be careful that your topic is not too specific. If you select a topic that is too specific, you will not need to give any examples to explain it. The topic for a paragraph of examples must be general enough to need several examples for its explanation. Note that in the topic sentences below, the focused topics are plural nouns (language*s*, park*s*, and sound*s*), and that there is a word in each sentence that means "multiple" (*several, some, certain*). This tells your reader that the paragraph will give examples.

Examples

For speakers of Spanish, there are several languages that are easy to learn.

Some of the parks in this city are especially entertaining for children.

When learning to speak English, French students find certain sounds difficult to pronounce.

When you write your example paragraph, use this list to check your topic sentence:

Topic Sentence Checklist (Paragraph of Examples)

__ 1. My topic will require several examples.

__ 2. My topic will interest the reader.

__ 3. My topic sentence has only one controlling idea.

Exercise 2.2 Look at the following topic sentence errors. With a partner (or as a class), rewrite each of the topic sentences correctly.

1. There are two ways to spell the words "color" and "odor." **(too specific and too boring)**

   Make this topic sentence more general and more interesting.

   _____

2. Argentina has solved many of its political problems, and it has many beautiful places for tourists to visit. **(has two controlling ideas)**

   Eliminate the extra controlling idea.

   _____

THE BODY

Using Concept Mapping to Generate Ideas

There are two ways to use a concept map to plan your example paragraph. You can decide on the main divisions of the support first, include them on your map, and then just brainstorm for those specific categories (see Exercise 2.5); or you can just brainstorm all of the examples you can think of, and then look at the map and categorize the examples like this:

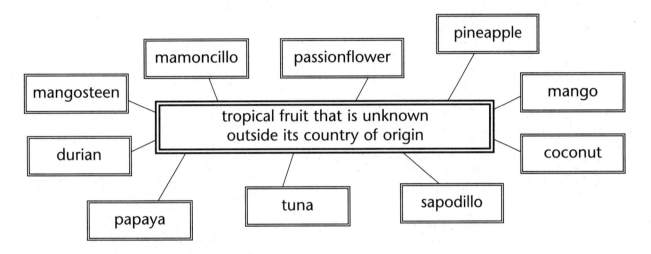

Category	Examples
Central and South America	mamoncillo, tuna, sapodillo
East India	mangosteen, durian
Australia	passionflower

Organizing Ideas (Categories and Examples)

Exercise 2.3 Sit with a partner for the following activity. Look at the example on pages 28 and 29, and then do the exercises that follow the example. Add details to the following concept map. In some of the exercises, the categories have already been chosen for you, but you may eliminate some or all and make your own categories. Do not change the topic, however.

Remember that the purpose of a concept map is to help you think and to organize your paragraph before you write.

Example

1. You see:

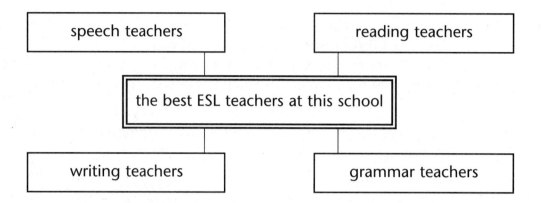

2. You write examples of each category:

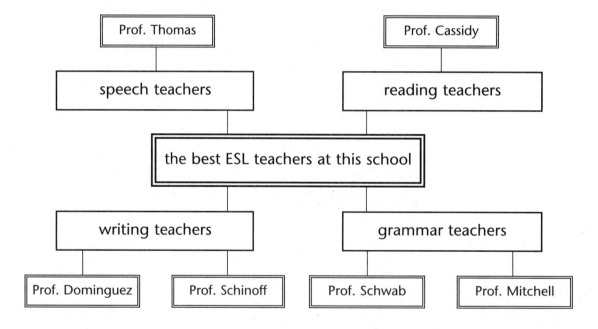

3. Then you write the topic sentence:

   Most of the teachers at my school are good, but there are some who are outstanding in their fields.

4. You list the best supporting ideas from your concept map:

Category	Examples
Writing teachers:	Prof. Dominguez and Prof. Schinoff
Reading teacher:	Prof. Cassidy
Grammar teachers:	Prof. Mitchell and Prof. Schwab
Speech teacher:	Prof. Thomas

Now you try it:

1. Decide which country you would like to write about, yours or your partner's. Discuss the economic, political, and social problems of that country.

2. Fill in the concept map below with examples of each category.

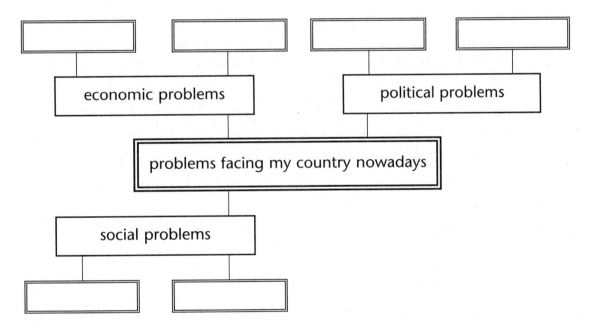

3. Write a topic sentence:

_____

_____

4. List the three best supporting ideas from your concept map:

Category   **Examples**

_____   _____

_____   _____

_____   _____

Exercise 2.4—Class Activity In small groups, pick **one of the three** options below. Follow the instructions for the topic you select. (Note that the second topic does not use categories on the concept map plan.)

Option #1

1. Use the topic (spouse qualities) and controlling idea (perfect) to create a concept map, and write a topic sentence. First, discuss the topic with your group. Then select three or four categories of examples and write them on the concept map. Next, list some interesting examples for each of your categories on the concept map. Then write the complete topic sentence, and put the supporting ideas (categories with their examples) in a logical order. Make sure all of the members of your group have the same information on the map, the same topic sentence, and the same supporting idea list. You will need them for a later assignment.

2. Write a topic sentence:

_____

_____

3. List the three best supporting ideas from your concept map:

Category   **Examples**

_____   _____

_____   _____

_____   _____

Option #2

1. Use the topic (wars) and controlling idea (famous) to create a concept map, and write a topic sentence. First, discuss the topic with your group. This time do NOT try to think of the categories first. Just write the names of all the famous wars you can think of. Look at your list of famous wars and discuss with your classmates how to categorize the examples. If you cannot think of any categories, then think of a logical way to organize the body of your paragraph. On the lines that follow the concept map, write the complete topic sentence, and put the supporting ideas in a logical order. Make sure all of the members of your group have the same information on the map, the same topic sentence, and the same supporting idea list. You will need them for a later assignment.

2. Write a topic sentence:

   _____

   _____

3. List the three best supporting ideas from your concept map:

   Category   **Examples**

   _____   _____

   _____   _____

   _____   _____

Option #3

1. Use the topic (disasters) and controlling idea (natural) to create a concept map, and write a topic sentence. First, discuss the topic with your group. Then select three or four categories of examples and write them on the concept map. Next, list some interesting examples for each of your categories on the concept map. On the lines that follow the concept map, write the complete topic sentence, and put the supporting ideas (categories with their examples) in a logical order. Make sure all of the members of your group have the same information on the map, the same topic sentence, and the same supporting idea list. You will need them for a later assignment.

2. Write a topic sentence:

   _____

   _____

3. List the three best supporting ideas from your concept map:

Category   **Examples**

_____   _____

_____   _____

_____   _____

Writing the Body of the Paragraph

In the previous exercise, you learned to generate ideas for a paragraph and to organize them, either in categories or as a list. The order of your main idea sentences in the body of the paragraph is flexible. You may put your most important category first or last. In this kind of paragraph, you can use your own judgment as to what you want to present first and last.

If you use categories to organize your support, you need to introduce each category in the body of the paragraph, and then write another sentence or two with the examples.

Look at the examples of categories and examples below and then read the paired sentences that follow. The first of each pair is a "main support" sentence. It contains a transition word or expression and introduces a new category in the body. The second of each pair gives the examples of the category. Can you see the difference between the "category" and the "examples"?

Topic and Controlling Idea	Categories	Examples
useful electrical devices found at home	used in the kitchen	microwave, coffee pot, oven, toaster
	used in living rooms	telephones, television, stereo
	used in bedrooms	radios, clocks

For the first supporting detail:

…First, there are some important electrical devices you can find in modern American kitchens. For example, many kitchens have a coffee pot, an oven, and a toaster, and some even have a microwave oven.

For the second or third supporting detail:

… Some very helpful and entertaining electrical devices can also be found in most living rooms. The television and stereo, for instance, entertain people and help them relax in the evenings.

For the last supporting detail:

… Finally, one last room where popular electrical devices can usually be seen is the bedroom. Most people keep alarm clocks and radios in their bedrooms, and some people also have televisions there.

Exercise 2.5 With a classmate, use the following information to create three pairs of sentences like those in the examples above.

Topic and Controlling Idea	Categories	Examples
international students in this writing course	from South America	Bolivians, Venezuelans, Colombians
	from Africa	South Africans, Ethiopians, Egyptians
	from Asia	Japanese, Vietnamese, Chinese

1. _____

_____

2. _____

_____

3. _____

_____

• Sentence Patterns for the Body of the Paragraph

1. Adjective Clauses

One way to add descriptive details to the support in your paragraph is to use adjective clauses (also called **relative clauses**). Adjective clauses will also help you avoid repetitiveness. If you write more than one sentence to describe or talk about the same noun, you can frequently change the additional sentence into an adjective clause and combine it with the main sentence (the sentence which names the noun).

Adjective clauses are dependent clauses, not complete sentences. They modify, describe, identify, or give information about a noun. Look at the following examples and try to do the exercises that follow. If you have difficulty writing adjective clauses, study the Chapter 2 Supplement on page 161.

Examples of Adjective Clauses

There is the math teacher. That math teacher teaches Algebra 101.

> There is the math teacher **who teaches Algebra 101.**

The teacher is in the hospital. We sent a "get well" card to that teacher.

> The teacher **to whom we sent a "get well"** card is in the hospital.

Algebra 101 is taught in room 3121. Algebra 101 is not a difficult math class.

> Algebra 101, **which is not a difficult math class,** is taught in room 3121.

She is a singer. That singer has written dozens of very popular songs.

> She is a singer **who has written dozens of very popular songs.**

Mark is the student. His car was stolen last week.

> Mark is the student **whose car was stolen last week.**

This is the city. I was born in this city.

> This is the city **where I was born.**

That was the time. We bought our first house then.

> That was the time **when we bought our first house.**

Exercise 2.6 Complete these sentences with (an) appropriate and logical adjective clause(s). Use *who, whom,* or *which.* Watch punctuation. For help, refer to the Chapter 2 Supplement.

Example

Teenagers...like music...

Teenagers ___who are rebelling against their parents___ like music ___which is loud.___

1. Do you like teachers...

   _____

2. All of the students...prefer to take tests...

   _____

3. Do you know anyone...

   _____

4. I would love to have a friend...

   _____

5. Patients...prefer doctors...

   _____

6. Students...like teachers...

   _____

7. Steven and Mark...like to eat at restaurants...

   _____

8. Do you prefer to read books...or books...

   _____

9. I admire people...

   _____

2. Transitional Expressions

Transitional Expressions		
for example (e.g.)	**for instance**	**such as**

In the body of your paragraph, you should use a transitional word or expression to tell your reader that you have finished one idea and are now going to begin another. If you do not use transitional words, your reader may have a difficult time understanding how the ideas in the body of your paragraph relate to each other, and your paragraph will probably sound choppy. For a more complete list of transitional words and expressions, with examples, exercises, and rules for punctuation, see Appendix 2.

Now we will look at a few transitional expressions used in paragraphs of illustration and example: *for example, e.g., for instance,* and *such as.* Except for *such as,* these transitional expressions follow the same rules of punctuation as other transitional words. They may NOT be used in an incomplete sentence. *For example* means the same as *e.g. (e.g.* is the abbreviation of the Latin phrase *exempli gratia),* but *e.g.* is usually preceded by a semicolon when connecting independent clauses.[1] Look at the following sentences.

Wrong: Some of the most popular fruits grow on trees. **For example,** mangoes and oranges.
FRAGMENT!!

Wrong: Some of the most popular fruits grow on trees. **E.g.,** mangoes and oranges.
FRAGMENT!!

Wrong: Other fruits grow on long stalks. **For instance,** bananas.
FRAGMENT!!

Corrections

Some of the most popular fruits, **for example,** mangoes and oranges, grow on trees. Other fruits, **for instance,** bananas, grow on long stalks.

Some of the most popular fruits, **e.g.,** mangoes and oranges, grow on trees. Other fruits, **for instance,** bananas, grow on long stalks.

Some of the most popular fruits, **for instance,** mangoes and oranges, grow on trees. Other fruits, **for instance,** bananas, grow on long stalks.

Several kinds of fruits grow well in subtropical climates. **For instance,** some of the most popular subtropical fruits, mangoes and oranges, come from South Florida.

Several kinds of fruits grow well in subtropical climates. **For example,** some of the most popular subtropical fruits, mangoes and oranges, come from South Florida.

---

1 Ask your instructor if he or she wants you to use *e.g.* in your writing (writing teachers sometimes discourage abbreviations).

Several kinds of fruits grow well in subtropical climates; **e.g.,** some of the most popular subtropical fruits, mangoes and oranges, come from South Florida.

Such as

Such as is also used to introduce an example, but not in the same way as a transitional expression. It cannot be followed by a complete sentence.

Wrong: It can be used in many ways, **such as** it can be boiled, baked, or fried.

Look at the three correct sentence patterns for *such as:*

Breakfast cereals can be made from a variety of grains, **such as** wheat and oats.

Several varieties of grain, **such as** wheat and oats, are used to make breakfast cereals.

Such varieties of grain **as** wheat and oats are used to make breakfast cereals.

Grains **such as** wheat and oats are used to make breakfast cereals.

Exercise 2.7 Write complete sentences using the words in parentheses as the examples. Use the underlined words to connect the clauses.

1. There are valuable gems in that jewelry store on the corner. (emeralds, diamonds, rubies, sapphires)

   a. *for example*

   _____

   b. *for instance*

   _____

   c. *such as*

   _____

   d. *e.g.*

   _____

2. Some semiprecious stones are as beautiful as precious stones. (jasper, agates)

   a. *for example*

   _____

   b. *for instance*

   _____

c. *such as*

_____

d. *e.g.*

_____

3. All "organic gems" come from living organisms.   (coral, pearls, amber)

   a. *for example*

   _____

   b. *for instance*

   _____

   c. *such as*

   _____

   d. *e.g.*

   _____

Exercise 2.8   Add these words to the paragraph below. (Refer to Appendix 2 for help.) Then write a conclusion for the paragraph.

in addition furthermore last but not least	for instance for example	or and

On the islands in the South Pacific, the breadfruit tree serves many important purposes. (1) _____ , the fruit of the tree is the main source of starch in the native diet. It can be eaten many different ways; (2) _____ , it can be roasted, sun-dried, fried, ground into flour, baked, (3) _____ boiled. (4) _____ , cloth is made from the inner bark of the tree. The fibers from that bark are removed (5) _____ woven to make beautiful clothes. (6) _____ , furniture and small boats can be made from the wood of the tree. These boats are used for transporting goods from island to island. (7) _____ , the sap from the stem of the breadfruit tree is used to make glue. (8) _____

Discuss: Is there a typical fruit or vegetable in your own country that you have not been able to find in this country? Describe it.

Exercise 2.9 Either by yourself or with a classmate, select one of the topics from Exercise 2.4 and write a paragraph about it. Be sure that the body has at least three supporting ideas and three adjective clauses, and that each supporting idea has two sentences: one that introduces the category, and a second (at least) that gives the examples for that category.

_____

_____

_____

_____

_____

_____

Exercise 2.10 Choose another topic from anywhere in this chapter, and plan and write a paragraph about it using examples as support. Include at least three adjective clauses and three transitional expressions that show examples *(for example, for instance, such as)* in the body. After you finish your paragraph, check it for the following details (except #6). Then read it aloud to yourself and then to a friend.

Checklist for Paragraph (Examples)

___   1. The paragraph has an interesting topic sentence.

___   2. The topic is not too specific. (In the topic sentence, the focused topic is a plural noun.)

___   3. The topic sentence has a controlling idea.

___   4. The body has at least three supporting ideas (examples).

___   5. The sentences in the body contain connecting words.

___   6. The paragraph has a conclusion.

THE CONCLUSION

As you have already learned, a good conclusion makes your paragraph sound finished. Your conclusion should not repeat your topic sentence word for word, nor should it contain any additional support. It concludes your idea by showing your purpose for writing the paragraph.

The kind of conclusion you write for an example paragraph depends on your purpose. If you write examples to persuade your audience, the conclusion could be advice or a suggestion. If your purpose was to inform the audience, then the conclusion could be an opinion, an invitation, or a restatement of the topic sentence.

Exercise 2.11 Read the following paragraph with a partner and write two different conclusions for it.

GAMES CHILDREN PLAY

Many games that children in the United States play help them develop physical and social skills. For example, games that make children run, jump, bend, and squat, such as tag or hide-and-go-seek, can increase a child's physical stamina and help the child keep fit and trim. Games like marbles and hopscotch, on the other hand, can help the child develop hand-eye coordination and can increase fine motor skills. Other games such as jump rope, tug-of-war, and freeze tag teach children to work in cooperation with others.

1. _____

_____

2. _____

_____

Exercise 2.12

1. Write a new conclusion for the paragraph that you wrote for Exercise 2.9.

2. Take two paragraphs from your work in this chapter (your own, the book's, or a classmate's) and write two different conclusions for each one. Copy (or photocopy) each paragraph once, and add the conclusions below each copy.

Exercise 2.13 Select a topic from Exercise 2.4 that you did *not* do with a classmate. Plan and write the new paragraph with a classmate. Use adjective clauses and transitional expressions in the body. Write a conclusion for your paragraph.

_____

_____

_____

_____

_____

Exercise 2.14 Using the paragraph, "Games Children Play," as a model, write a paragraph on your own paper about the games children play in your own country. Use adjective clauses and transitional words and expressions in the body.

EDITING SYMBOLS

Problems with Sentences: Grammar and Syntax (*ps, wo, ss*)

● Parallel Structure (*ps*)

Symbol	Meaning	Explanation
ps	Parallel structure	Some elements in the sentence do not have parallel structure.

Examples

Wrong: I like to **swim,** fishing and jogging.
             ps

Correction: I like **swimming, fishing,** and **jogging.**

Wrong: She writes clearly and **in a neat way.**
                                    ps

Correction: She writes **clearly and neatly.**

When you write a sentence that has compound structures, items in a series, or a list, or when you write an outline, the structures must have the same grammatical structure.

Example

Wrong: **Studying** your notes, **following** the test instructions carefully, and **to write** the responses clearly can help you pass the tests in your courses.

Correction: **Studying** your notes, **following** the test instructions carefully, and **writing** the responses clearly can help you pass the tests in your courses.

Exercise 2.15 With a partner, correct the *ps* errors in the following sentences.

1. Dogs, cats, and owning birds can be good house pets.
   ps

   _____

   _____

2. Some computer programs are hard to find, difficult to install, and you cannot run them easily.   *ps*

   _____

   _____

3. Always use blue or black ink, double-space your paragraphs, and your work should be turned in on time.   *ps*

   _____

   _____

4. You can go to the library to check out books, research a topic, or to read current magazines.   *ps*

   _____

   _____

5. I watched the television program that they had recommended and which was on channel 6.   *ps*

   _____

   _____

Exercise 2.16   Find three **parallel structure errors** in the assignments that have been returned to you, and analyze them as follows.

Example

Error: The class was listening to the teacher and wrote notes about the lecture.

***ps* problem:** I mixed verb tenses and used past continuous with simple past in the same sentence.

Rule: With compound structures, you must use the same grammar form.

Correction: The class was listening to the teacher and writing notes about the lecture.

● Word Order *(wo)*

Symbol	Meaning	Explanation
wo	Word order	The words in the sentence are in the wrong order.

Examples

Wrong: Give to me the ball blue.
                                    wo

Correction: Give me the blue ball.

This symbol indicates that some of the words in your sentence are in the wrong place. Students can make this error when they translate directly from their native language into English.

Exercise 2.17   Correct the *wo* errors in the following sentences.

Example

That house large and green belongs to the uncle of Tom.
   That large green house belongs to Tom's uncle.

1. I gave to Mary the book, and she gave to Harry a notebook of Mark.
      wo   *wo*   *wo*

2. We have money enough to buy the car new now.
   wo   *wo*

   _____

3. Never they pay the rent on time.
   wo

   _____

4. In the United States, people have a life very busy most days of the week.
                                                          wo

   _____

5. As you know, many young people when they come here from their own country
   feel frustrated.   *wo*

   _____

6. They'll more obey their owners.
   wo

   _____

Exercise 2.18 Find three **word order errors** in the assignments that have been returned to you, and analyze them as follows.

Example

Error: _I gave the book blue to Mary._____

***wo* problem:** _I put my adjective after my noun._____

Rule: _Adjectives go in front of nouns or after linking verbs._____

Correction: _I gave the blue book to Mary._____

● Sentence Structure (*ss*)

Symbol	Meaning	Explanation
ss	Sentence structure	The sentence structure contains an error.

Examples

Wrong: Due to it is raining, we won't go.
ss

Correction: Due to the rain, we won't go.

Wrong: She is absent because of she is sick.
ss

Correction: She is absent because she is sick.

This symbol on your paper indicates that your sentence does not follow English sentence structure. You may need to look up the grammar structure to correct the mistake. Ask your teacher for help if you need an explanation of your *ss* errors. You might have to explain to your teacher in other words what you were trying to write.

Exercise 2.19 With a partner, discuss the *ss* errors in the following sentences. If possible, try to correct some of the sentences (you choose). This will be difficult if you cannot understand what the author was trying to say.

1. Their similarities make a good friendship they have. *ss*

   _____

2. Another characteristic in common is kind of person. *ss*

   _____

3. Cars are different from motorcycles in that while cars are faster than motorcycles. *ss*

   _____

4. Unlike my brother, who is much taller than my sister. *ss*

   _____

5. Zuleika and I have difficult in many ways. *ss*

   _____

6. Life in the United States and life in Bolivia are similar because they have the same style of life in that both have a large variety of people and a large society. *ss*

   _____

   _____

7. It is sometimes better to know it than does not know it. *ss*

Exercise 2.20 Find two **sentence structure errors** in the assignments that have been returned to you, and analyze them as follows.

Example

Error: Bogota and Medellin are similar with Cartagena with geography.

ss problem: I mixed different kinds of sentence patterns.

Rule: "Similar" needs "to." "With respect to" can have a noun after it. "With" is not enough.

Correction: Bogota and Medellin are similar to Cartegena with respect to their geography.

chapter
three

Paragraphs of Comparison

The computer program that accompanies the editing symbols in this chapter is called: **Chapter 3—Disk 1**

Discuss:

1. What is the difference between a "comparison" and a "contrast"?

2. When you write a comparison or a contrast, is it possible to write about only one topic? For example, could you "compare your sister"? Why not?

3. Are there some topics that would not be good for a comparison paragraph? For example, would it be easy for you to describe the **similarities** between a dog and a pencil? Would it be interesting to read about the **similarities** between a white pencil and a blue pencil?

4. What makes a good topic for a comparison paragraph?

5. With a partner, list five possible topics for a comparison paragraph. You can use people, places, things, or ideas.

   Example

   similarities between Colombia (my partner's country) and Venezuela (my country)

   a. _____

   b. _____

   c. _____

   d. _____

   e. _____

INTRODUCTION AND MODEL PARAGRAPHS

In a comparison paragraph, you write about the similarities between two or more things or groups of things. The topic sentence tells your reader what you are going to compare. The body of your paragraph contains the comparison. The conclusion usually tells why you compared them; it gives your opinion, some advice, a suggestion, or an invitation, or it restates the topic sentence using different words. In this chapter, you will learn how to plan a paragraph of comparison and about sentence structures, or patterns, that will help you write the topic sentence and support sentences for your comparison paragraph. You will also practice writing conclusions to comparison paragraphs.

Exercise 3.1   Read the following comparison paragraph with a partner. Underline all of the words you can find that show comparison. The first sentence is an example.

My mother is **like** my father **in that both** enjoy a quiet lifestyle. For example, my parents live near the ocean, and they love to take long walks by the sea in the morning. They both love the quiet sunrise on the ocean and the feel of the gentle breeze on their faces. In addition, they both have a profession that does not cause stress or anxiety. They own a nursery and spend their days making things grow. Like my mother, my father says that he feels peaceful when working among healthy growing plants. That feeling of peace is evident in my parents' home as well. For example, after a dinner consisting of homegrown vegetables and brown rice, both of my parents like to listen to classical music and to read books. My father enjoys books written by Native Americans that teach people to live in harmony with nature, and my mother does, too. I have learned a lot from my parents, and I hope to find a lifestyle as peaceful as theirs when I marry.

Discuss: Does this lifestyle appeal to you (sound good to you)? Why? Why not? What do you think your future lifestyle will be like?

GENERATING IDEAS

Brainstorming for Details

Exercise 3.2

1. List the similarities (not the differences) between your **mother** and your **father** using the categories below.

Category Examples	Comparison
personality	Both are optimistic and happy.
physical characteristics	Both have brown hair and eyes.
hobbies and interests	Both love to travel, cook, and read.
nationality and race	Both are French.
religion	no similarity
treatment of you	Both love me very much.

educational background	Both are college graduates.
professions	no similarity
other?	Both speak three languages.

Category	Comparison
personality	_____
physical characteristics	_____
hobbies and interests	_____
nationality and race	_____
religion	_____
treatment of you	_____
educational background	_____
professions	_____
other?	_____

2. Sit with a partner and compare **two people in this class** who seem very similar to each other. Talk about how they are similar, and then list their similarities. You can add more categories if you want.

Category	Comparison
personality	_____
type of student they are	_____
behavior in class	_____
nationality	_____
physical characteristics	_____
ability in English	_____
style of dress / hair	_____
other?	_____

3. Think about your best friend. How are **you** and **your best friend** similar?

Category   **Comparison**

_____   _____

_____   _____

_____   _____

_____   _____

_____   _____

_____   _____

_____   _____

_____   _____

_____   _____

4. If you could create **the ideal mate** for yourself, what similarities would you like him/her to share with you?

Category   **Comparison**

_____   _____

_____   _____

_____   _____

_____   _____

_____   _____

_____   _____

_____   _____

_____   _____

_____   _____

Organizing the Details

Look at the following paragraph, and answer the questions that follow it.

Ronny and Steve have a lot in common. For example, they share a similar **cultural background.** Both Ronny and Steve are from Cuba, and both of them have parents who were born in Germany. Thus they both speak Spanish and German and enjoy German and Cuban food. Another amazing similarity between Ronny and Steve is their **hobbies.** Both boys are interested in underwater photography and deep-sea diving. In fact, they both frequently go diving in the ocean to take underwater pictures. Ronny and Steve also have the same kind of **personality.** They are outgoing, enjoy meeting new people, and are popular among their friends. As you can see, Ronny and Steve have a lot in common; in fact, they recently realized that they share so many interests and get along so well that they have decided to become roommates in college next year.

Exercise 3.3

1. Which words in the topic sentence tell the reader that the paragraph will be a comparison?

2. How many sentences are there in this paragraph?

3. List the three main categories in the body of this paragraph (they are in **boldface** print).

    a. _____

    b. _____

    c. _____

4. Add the categories and the details (the actual similarities) that are in the body of the paragraph to this concept map. This is a good technique to use for organizing your support for paragraphs of comparison.

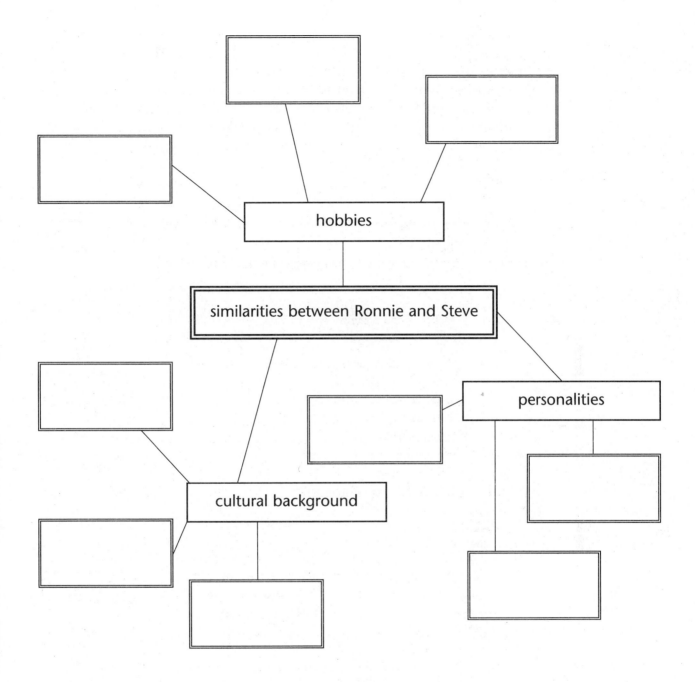

Exercise 3.4 Add details to the two concept maps on the following pages. Each detail must be something that both topics have in common. Some of the categories have already been chosen for you, but you may eliminate some or all and make your own categories. Remember that the purpose of a concept map is to help you think and to organize your paragraph before you write. After you write the details for the map, you will write a topic sentence, and list the details for a comparison paragraph.

Example

Audience and Purpose: Your fiancé(e) is working in another country. He/She has asked you to write and tell him/her about your parents. You have decided to focus on the positive aspects as you compare the similarities between your mother and your father because you want your fiancé(e) to like your parents. Follow the example below to plan your paragraph.

1. You see:

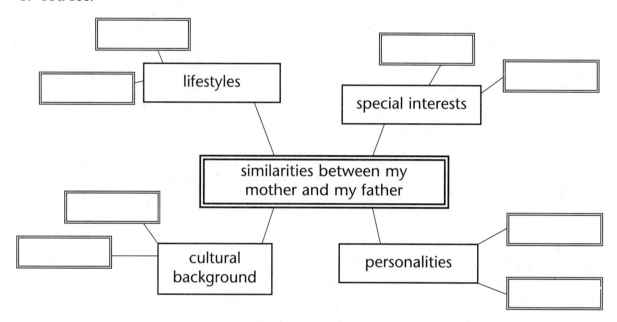

2. You add similarities (details for comparison).

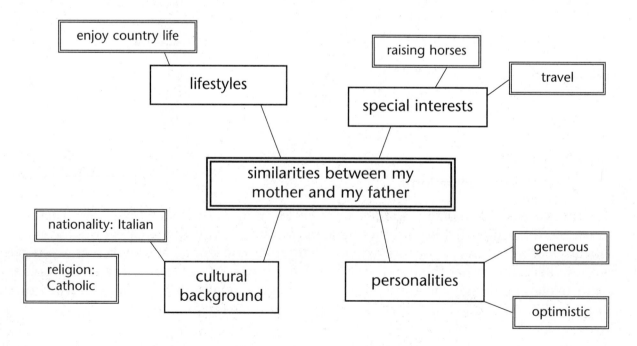

3. Then write the topic sentence:

There are many wonderful similarities between my mother and my father.

4. Finally, choose and list the three best supporting categories with the similarities (details for comparison) from your concept map.

Category	Comparison
cultural background	Both are Italian and both are Catholic.
personality	Both are optimistic and generous.
lifestyles	Both love the quiet life of the country.

Now you do it!

1.

Audience and Purpose: Your teacher will be moving with her family to your country next year and wants to know about the educational system there. You decide to describe it by comparing it to the system in this country.

1. Study the following concept map.

2. Add details to the concept map.

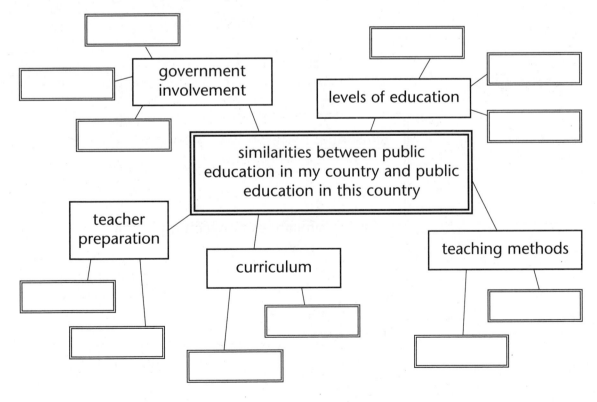

3. Write the topic sentence: _____

_____

4. List the three best supporting ideas from your concept map and add secondary support as needed.

Category   **Comparison**

_____   _____

_____   _____

_____   _____

2.

Audience and Purpose: You are writing about two important cities in your home town for a friend who works in a travel agency. The description will be published in your friend's travel magazine, so you want to focus on the positive aspects of the two cities.

1. Study the following concept map.

2. Add details to the concept map.

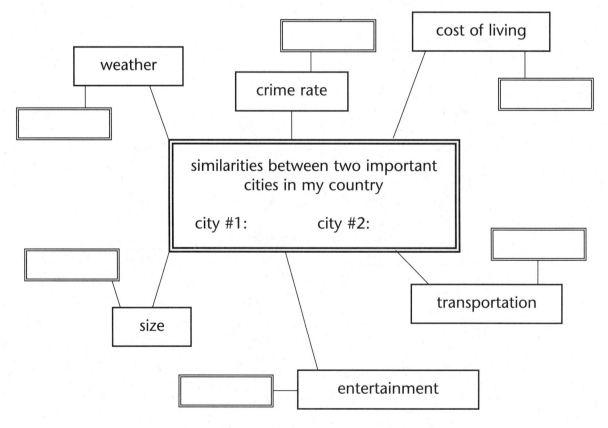

3. Write the topic sentence: _____

_____

4. List the three best supporting ideas from your concept map:

Category   **Comparison**

_____   _____

_____   _____

_____   _____

Exercise 3.5 With a partner (or alone if you prefer), use the following concept map as a model. On a separate piece of paper, plan a comparison paragraph. First select a topic from the discussion question #5 on page 48 of this chapter. Select an audience and a purpose for your paragraph. Write a topic sentence. Then choose three or four categories for the body of your comparison, and write them in the concept map. Next write a comparison for each category. Save this work. You will use it in two assignments later in this chapter.

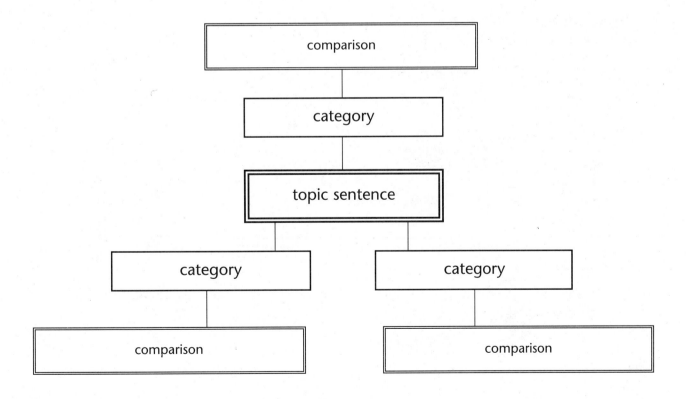

THE TOPIC SENTENCE

Introduction

In comparison paragraphs you describe similarities. There are two **topics** in these paragraphs because your paragraph discusses how the **topics** are similar to one another. You should present both of these topics in the topic sentence. Also, make sure that your topic sentence is not too general, so your paragraph will not be boring, and that it informs the reader that your paragraph will discuss "similarities."

Even though the controlling idea for your comparison paragraph is "similar," you can add an adjective such as "unusual," "amazing," or "fascinating" to the topic sentence to give the paragraph an interesting aspect and to catch your reader's attention.

Read the topic sentences below. Discuss which sentence is the most boring, and why the other two sentences are more interesting.

Tom is similar to Steven in three ways.

Tom and Steven are similar.

Tom and Steven share some very strange similarities.

When you write your topic sentence, check for the following:

Topic Sentence Checklist
(Paragraph of Comparison)

__ 1. My topic is focused and interesting.

__ 2. I mentioned the aspects of the topic that I will compare.

__ 3. I wrote both topics in the sentence.

__ 4. I let my reader know that the paragraph will be a comparison.

__ 5. I wrote only one controlling idea.

Look at the following topic sentence errors. With a partner (or as a class), rewrite each of the topic sentences correctly.

1. Canada is similar to the United States in many ways. **(too general for one paragraph)**

   Make this topic sentence more specific.

   _____

2. Canada is very similar with respect to geography. **(only one topic is mentioned)**

Write this topic sentence with two topics.

_____

3. Canada and the United States are beautiful countries. **(not clear to reader that the paragraph will _compare_ the two countries.)**

Make this topic sentence introduce a comparison.

_____

4. Canada and the United States have similar landscapes for several reasons. **(mixes controlling ideas of "comparison" with "reasons")**

Eliminate the extra controlling idea.

_____

Sentence Patterns for Topic Sentences

Below are five sentence patterns you can use to write topic sentences of comparison. In the Chapter 3 Supplement, you will find more charts, examples, explanations, and exercises for each of the patterns.

If you do not need to focus your topic, you can use any one of the first three patterns below. How do you know if your topic does not need to be focused? Ask yourself if it sounds like your paragraph will interest your audience. If it does, then use one of these first three patterns.

Pattern #1

a. **(similar)** Although you may not believe it, the two strongest human emotions, love and hate, are **similar** in several ways.

b. **(alike)** Although you may not believe it, the two strongest human emotions, love and hate, are **alike** in several ways.

Pattern #2

a. **(similar to)** A hurricane is **similar to** a tornado in three dangerous ways.

b. **(like)** A hurricane is **like** a tornado in three important ways.

Pattern #3

There are many strange similarities **between** the deaths of Abraham Lincoln and John F. Kennedy.

If you need to focus your topic, you can use either of the two patterns below. These patterns do not use the word "ways." They name a focused topic. How do you know if you need to focus your topic? Just ask yourself, will this topic be interesting to my audience? Will it tell them something they don't know? If you see no purpose for your topic, you should focus it or change it.

Pattern #4

My aunt and my uncle **share** the same basic religious beliefs.

Pattern #5

My aunt is **similar to** my uncle **with respect to** religious beliefs.

Exercise 3.6 Do this exercise with a partner. Write topic sentences using the topics and sentence patterns as indicated.

1. my partner's country and my own country

    a. ...are similar in...

    _____

    b. ...is similar to...

    _____

    c. ...is like...

    _____

    d. There are...similarities

    _____

    e. ...share the same...

    _____

2. two classmates (not my partner or myself)

    a. ...are alike in...

    _____

    b. ...is similar to...

    _____

c. ...is like...

_____

d. There are...similarities

_____

e. ...have the same...

_____

3. a sea and a lake

   a. ...are similar in...

   _____

   b. ...is similar to...

   _____

   c. ...is like...

   _____

   d. There are...similarities

   _____

   e. ...share the same...

   _____

4. a hippopotamus and a rhinoceros

   a. ...are alike in...

   _____

   b. ...is similar to...

   _____

   c. ...is like...

   _____

   d. There are...similarities

   _____

   e. ...eat almost the same...

   _____

Exercise 3.7 With a classmate, rewrite each of the following boring topic sentences using one of the sentence patterns above.

1. Oranges and grapefruit are similar.

   _____

2. Lions and tigers are similar.

   _____

3. Coca-Cola is like Pepsi Cola.

   _____

4. An exam is similar to a quiz.

   _____

5. A watch and a clock are alike.

   _____

Exercise 3.8 Look at the topics you and your partner wrote in Exercise 3.5. Use the sentence patterns you have learned to write a topic sentence for the concept map. Keep the topic sentence because you will use it again in a later exercise.

_____

THE BODY OF THE COMPARISON PARAGRAPH

Introduction

The body of your paragraph must develop the topic sentence. If your topic sentence tells your reader that you will explain similarities, then you cannot describe differences in the paragraphs. If your topic sentence tells your reader that you will discuss physical similarities, then you cannot describe personality or attitudes. Look at the following paragraph. It mixes controlling ideas and does not develop the topic sentence.

Although my older brother and I do not seem very much alike, we both have a lot of physical similarities.[1] All our lives, our friends have told us that physically we look the same, but our personalities are totally different. First of all, my brother is always friendlier than I. He is the kind of person who can socialize with anybody. On the other hand, I am never like that. I am more attached to my family. I consider myself to be a very sentimental person, while my brother doesn't care about family problems. In conclusion, even though we are brothers, there are plenty of differences between us.

Discuss:

1. Does the topic sentence say that the paragraph will discuss similarities or differences?

2. Does the conclusion say that the paragraph discussed similarities or differences?

3. What did the paragraph discuss, similarities or differences?

4. The topic sentence says that the paragraph will describe only **physical similarities.** Does the paragraph do that?

5. How could you fix this paragraph?

When you write comparisons, you can organize the body of your paragraphs into three or more categories. These categories are usually nouns. They are in the main support sentences of the paragraph's body, and they tell the reader which aspect of your two topics you are going to compare. Then, a comparison is given in the next sentence or two (the **secondary support**).

In the following pages, you will learn to develop the body of your paragraph step by step. First, let's review the difference between the "category" and the "comparison." (You learned this in Chapter 3.) Look at the examples below.

Category	**Comparison**
level of difficulty	The midterm and the final are extremely difficult.
software programs	IBM and Macintosh use similar software programs.
level of intelligence	Tom and Mark are both quite intelligent.
height	My mother is almost as tall as my father.
location	Eureka and Arcata are near the ocean in the Sequoia National Forest.
speed	The Porsche can go just as fast as the Corvette.
price	Both cars cost the same.

---

1 The controlling idea is almost never written in the dependent clause. It is in the main clause of a sentence. To correct this topic sentence, write the second part (physical similarities) as the dependent clause and the first part (*...not much alike*) as the independent clause.

The sentences below were made from the information in the category and comparison lists above. The first of each pair of sentences below is a "main support" sentence. It contains a transition word or expression, and it tells the reader what will be compared. The second of each paired sentences gives the comparison.

To introduce the first supporting detail:

...First, both tests have the same **level of difficulty.** The midterm and the final are both so difficult that the students cannot pass them.

...One important similarity between the IBM and the Macintosh is that both use essentially the same **software programs.** The major software developers create programs such as PageMaker, Word, and Word MacroMind Director for both platforms.

To introduce the second or third supporting detail:

...Tom and Mark also have similar levels of **intelligence.** Both attend the university and do well in all their classes.

...Another similarity between my mother and my father is their **height.** My mother is almost as tall as my father.

...Yet another similarity between Eureka and Arcata is their **location**. Both towns are situated near the Pacific Ocean and are surrounded by the Sequoia National Forest.

...In addition, as far as **price** is concerned, the two cars are identical. Both cars cost $12,500.

To introduce the last supporting detail

...Finally, as far as **speed** is concerned, the two cars are alike. The Porsche can go just as fast as the Corvette.

The transitional expressions in the sentences above tell your reader that you have finished one idea and are now going to begin another. They make your paragraph easy to understand. If you do not use transition words, your reader may have a difficult time seeing how the ideas in the body of your paragraph relate to each other. Below are some sentence patterns you can use to announce a different supporting idea in a paragraph. You can find these and more in Appendix 2.

One important similarity between X and Y is...

First, X and Y both...

X and Y **also** [verb] similar [nouns]

As far as personality **is concerned**...

(Yet) another astonishing similarity between X and Y is…

In addition, as far as [noun] is concerned, both X and Y…

One last important similarity between X and Y…

Finally, as far as [noun] is concerned, X and Y…

Exercise 3.9 With a partner, rewrite the following paragraph. Add transitional words and expressions to introduce the three main supporting details.

The cheetah has certain features in common with its cousin the tiger. They are both wild animals living in the deep jungle, where they hunt and run freely. The cheetah eats meat, and so does the tiger. They search for other wild animals such as deer, zebras, and antelope to kill. They are not intimidated by their prey's sizes; when they are hungry, they will attack almost any living thing in order to survive. Their behavior is very similar. Both animals have strong tempers, and no animal can invade their territory, or they will react in self-defense. As you can see, the cheetah and the tiger are dangerous, and they are usually treated with great respect by the other animals in the jungle.

Exercise 3.10 With a partner, use the following information to write pairs of supporting sentences similar to those in the previous examples. The first sentence in each pair will introduce the category. Be sure to include the category and a transition word or expression in the first sentence. The second sentence will contain the comparison.

Category	Comparison	
a. form of government	Argentina is democratic.	Peru is democratic.
b. nationality	Leo comes from Uruguay.	Julio comes from Uruguay.
c. languages	Julie speaks French and Spanish.	Sally speaks French and Spanish.
d. physical appearance	Jenny is tall with long brown hair.	Marie is tall with long brown hair.

1. _____

2. _____

3. _____

4. _____

Sentence Patterns for the Body of the Paragraph

You can use the sentence patterns below in the body of your paragraph to introduce each support and to add secondary support to your main points. In the Chapter 3 Supplement, you will find more charts, explanations, examples, and exercises for each of the patterns.

Pattern #1

Jane wears almost **the same** hairstyle **as** Mary (does).

Pattern #2

a. Los Angeles is **similar to** New York **in that** both cities are near an ocean.

b. Los Angeles is **like** New York **in that** both cities are near an ocean.

Pattern #3

Like Francia, Adriana lives in Kendall with her family.

Pattern #4

a. John lives here, and **so** does Henry.

b. John lives here, and Henry does **too.**

c. (John lives here, **but** Henry doesn't.)

Pattern #5

a. John doesn't live here, and **neither** does Henry.

b. John doesn't live here, and Henry doesn't **either.**

c. (John lives here, **but** Henry doesn't.)

Pattern #6

Both you **and** I like to live here in South Florida. **Both** like to live here in South Florida.

Pattern #7

Neither you **nor** your sisters are here. **Neither** you **nor** your sister is here.

Exercise 3.11 Do this exercise with a partner. Write sentences using the topics and sentence patterns as indicated.

1. The U.S. / Canada / types of natural resources. **(Pattern #1)**

   _____

2. The symphony sounded marvelous. / The choir sounded marvelous. **(Pattern #4b)**

   _____

3. We wrote the paragraph quickly. / The conclusion was more difficult. **(Pattern #4c)**

   _____

4. The soup was delicious. / The sandwich was not delicious. **(Pattern #5c)**

   _____

5. The captain was here yesterday. / The lieutenant was here yesterday. **(Pattern #6)**

   _____

6. The radio did not report the crime. / The television didn't report the crime. **(Pattern #7)**

   _____

Exercise 3.12

1. Look at the concept map and lists that you developed in Exercise 3.4 #1 (similarities between public education in your country and in this country). Keeping your audience and the purpose of your paragraph in mind, use the sentence patterns above to write a paragraph. Then, ask a classmate to read it and tell you if it is interesting and easy to understand. Change the parts of the paragraph that your classmate does not understand.

2. Follow the instructions above for Exercise 3.4 #2.

THE CONCLUSION

The conclusion of your comparison paragraph must make the paragraph sound finished. It should make your reason for writing the comparison clear to your reader. In the concluding sentence, it is common to name the two topics again and then to offer an opinion, some advice, or an invitation to your reader.

Exercise 3.13 Take two paragraphs from your work in this chapter (your own, the book's, or a classmate's) and write two different conclusions for each one. Copy (or photocopy) each paragraph once, and write the new conclusions below each.

Exercise 3.14 Sit with the partner who helped you write the answers to discussion question #5 on page 48 of this chapter. Together, select one of the topics and write a paragraph of comparison. Use transitional words and expressions in the body of the paragraph, and use the sentence patterns you have learned in this chapter. Then write a conclusion for your paragraph.

Exercise 3.15 At home, write two paragraphs using the information you wrote in Exercise 1 (pick your favorite two from the list you developed in Exercise 3.2 on pages 49–51). Use transitional words and sentence patterns you learned in this chapter in your paragraphs. Then write a conclusion for your paragraph.

Exercise 3.16 Sit with the partner who helped you develop the ideas for the concept map in Exercise 3.5. Show each other your topic sentences from Exercise 3.8. Choose one of the topic sentences and use the information in the map to write the body of the paragraph. Use several of the sentence patterns presented in this chapter (see the Chapter 3 Supplement for more help with sentence patterns). Write a conclusion to the paragraph.

Exercise 3.17 How many errors can you find in the following paragraph (there are more than 10)? Underline each error, correct it, and then rewrite the paragraph correctly. Some of the errors are in punctuation, sentence structure, subject-verb agreement, word form, and wrong words. There are also some serious paragraph errors. Ask yourself the following questions:

1. Is the paragraph interesting? Do you learn anything interesting from the paragraph?

2. Is the conclusion good? (Compare it to the topic sentence.)

(1) Miami and Cuba has several characteristics in common. (2) First, Miami has almost the same weather like Cuba, Miami is always hot, and also Cuba is. (3) Another characteristic in common is kinds of people, Miami has the same kinds of people like Cuba, the people in Miami are friendly and honest, and in Cuba the people are friendly and honest too. (4) The last characteristic in common is style of life, in Miami, everybody works, dances, sings, and plays sports. (5) And in Cuba, everybody working, dancing, singing, and playing sports. (6) As you can see, Miami and Cuba have several characteristics in common.

EDITING SYMBOLS

Problems with Sentence Grammar and Syntax (*agr*)

● **Three Agreement Errors**

Symbol	Meaning	Explanation
sv agr	Subject-verb agreement	The subject and verb do not agree in number.

Examples

      Wrong: He go early to class on Mondays.
              sv agr

Correction: He goes to class early on Mondays.

      Wrong: Everyone know the answer now.
                 sv agr

Correction: Everyone knows the answer now.

With all verbs except *be,* the present and present perfect verb tenses end in *-s* in the third person singular (*he, she, it*). Words such as "one," "each," and "every" are sometimes separated from the main verb by a prepositional phrase with plural nouns, but they are singular, and the verb must agree with them.

Exercise 4.18 Correct the *agr* errors in the following sentences:

1. One of the students in this class have my book.
                                    agr

_____

2. Every one of the senators need to vote for the bill.
                               agr

_____

3. Each of the students have his or her own personalized exam.
                        agr

_____

4. Everybody like to live in tropical climates, until there is a hurricane.

   agr

   _____

5. I think one of our teachers were in that accident.

   agr

   _____

Symbol	Meaning	Explanation
pron agr	Pronoun agreement	The pronoun does not agree with the subject.

Examples

Wrong: Everyone likes to have **their** own car.
             pron agr

Correction: Everyone likes to have **his** or **her** own car.

Wrong: Everyone did **his** homework last night.
          pron agr

Correction: Everyone did **his** or **her** homework last night.

Although it is possible to correct the above error by using "his or her," "he or she," or "him or her," it sounds awkward. You can avoid the problem by using plurals or by eliminating the pronouns.

Wrong: Everyone like to have **their** own car.
           pron agr

Correction: Everyone likes to have **his** or **her** own car.

Better Correction: People like to have **their** own cars.

Wrong: Everyone did **his** homework last night.
          pron agr

Correction: Everyone did **his** or **her** homework last night.

Better Correction: Everyone did **the** homework last night.

Also be sure that you know the sex of your subject, and use the appropriate masculine or feminine pronoun in your sentence.

Wrong: John goes to **her** job early.
pron agr

Correction: John goes to **his** job early.

The pronouns *everyone, everybody, anyone, one,* and *no one* are singular, so when you use pronouns to replace these words, the pronouns must also be singular. (Don't use the impersonal "you" in academic writing.)

Exercise 3.19

With a partner, correct all of the agreement errors in the following sentences:

1. Everyone like to enjoy their weekend activities at that club.
   agr   agr

   _____

2. Have everyone finished their test?
   agr   agr

   _____

3. I don't think anyone have bought their class textbook yet.
   agr   agr

   _____

4. One need to prepare for their next vacations right now.
   agr   agr

   _____

Symbol	Meaning	Explanation
# agr	Number agreement	The word is plural and should be singular or vice versa.

Examples

Wrong: These book are mine.
 # agr

Correction: These books are mine.

Wrong: There's solutions to every problems.
 # agr

Correction: There are solutions to all problems. (or every problem)

The pronoun that you use to replace a noun is plural if the noun was plural and singular if the noun was singular. Also, be careful of "this," "these," "that," and "those." If you use a plural form of the demonstrative adjective *(these, those)*, then you must have a plural noun. All adjectives in English have the same form for singular and plural.

Exercise 3.20 With a partner correct the *agr* errors in the following sentences:

1. There's always people who steal from stores. These makes the prices of the
   agr   *agr*

   merchandise go up for everyone.

   _____

2. The two animals have several similarity.
                                      agr

   _____

3. Do you think there's many people who believe he is innocent?
                     agr

   _____

4. Life in the United States and life in Perú has several similarity.
                                            agr   *agr*

   _____

Exercise 3.21 Find three **agreement errors** in the assignments which have been returned to you, and analyze them as follows.

Example

Error: Bogota and Medellin is beautiful.
_____

***agr* problem:** I used a singular verb with a plural noun.
_____

Rule: Plural subjects need plural verbs.
_____

Correction: Bogota and Medellin are beautiful.
_____

chapter
four

Paragraphs of Contrast

The computer programs that accompany the editing symbols in this chapter are called: **Chapter 4—Disk 1** and **Chapter 4—Disk 2**

INTRODUCTION AND MODEL PARAGRAPH

The contrast paragraph is similar to the comparison paragraph (Chapter 3). In the comparison paragraph, you describe **similarities** between at least two things; in a contrast paragraph, you write about the **differences** between at least two things. The topic sentence tells the reader what you are going to contrast, the body contrasts several aspects of the two topics, and the conclusion finishes the contrast with your opinion, some advice, or an invitation.

Exercise 4.1 Read the model paragraph below. Underline all of the expressions that show contrast.

> Even though Ron and Steve are brothers, they have almost nothing in common. The most obvious difference is that **they do not look at all like brothers.** Ron is tall and thin with blond hair and a clear complexion, while Steve is short and stocky with dark hair and freckles. The two boys also have very different **personalities.** Ron is friendlier and more outgoing than Steve. In fact, Steve is shy and avoids meeting strangers. As far as **school** is concerned, Steve is a much more serious student than his brother. Ron enjoys playing sports, but he doesn't like to take difficult classes. On the other hand, Steve is active in academic activities such as editing the school newspaper, and he belongs to the math and computer clubs. This is why Steve usually gets better grades than his brother. As you can imagine, Ron and Steve are so different from one another that most people do not believe they are related at all.

1. Does the paragraph show similarities or differences?

2. List the other two main categories of the paragraph here (the first is an example):

    a. __what they look like (physical appearance)__

    b. _____

    c. _____

Even though the paragraph structure for the comparison and the contrast paragraph is similar in many ways, there is one important difference. In a comparison, both subjects **share** common characteristics, so the sentences in the body of the paragraph are relatively simple.

Examples

Both Jane and Susan are **from the same country—Honduras.**

Jane and Susan have similar interests. **Both enjoy swimming and jogging.**

In a contrast paragraph, however, the subjects do not share characteristics, and the differences between the two subjects must be carefully and completely explained. This makes the sentences in a contrast paragraph more complex.

Examples

Jane and Susan are from different countries. While **Jane** is *from Mexico,* a country with a temperate climate, **Susan** is *from Canada,* which overall has a cool climate.

Jane and Susan do not share the same interests. **Jane** loves *swimming and hiking.* **Susan,** however, *enjoys sewing and cooking.*

In this chapter, you will learn about sentence patterns to use to write contrasts, and a concept map technique to help you plan complete contrasts.

Exercise 4.2 Read the previous paragraph again, and look at the concept map below. The categories *school, physical appearance,* and *personality* are the first **branches** of the concept map. Find the details for each of these categories in the body of the paragraph, and add them to the map.

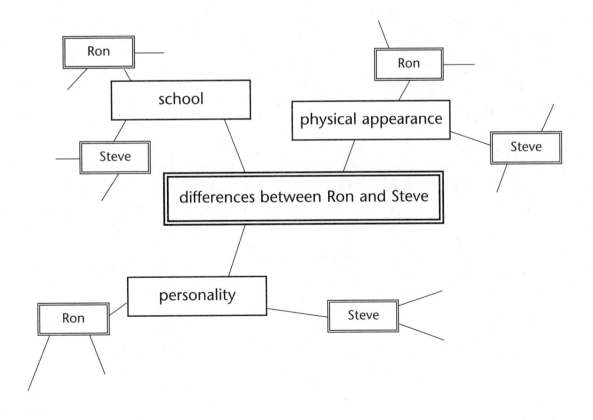

● ● ● ● ● ● ● ● ● ● ● ● ● ●
GENERATING IDEAS

Exercise 4.3

1. Look around your classroom and try to locate the classmate who is the most different from you. Ask that person to be your partner. You will interview each other and try to find out all of the ways in which you are different from each other. Using the same type of list that you did for comparisons, fill in the **contrasting** details. Keep this information because you will need it for a later exercise.

Category	My Partner	Myself
nationality	_____	_____
future goals	_____	_____
hobbies and interests	_____	_____
age, family, marital status	_____	_____
physical characteristics	_____	_____
cultural or religious background	_____	_____
lifestyle	_____	_____
other _____	_____	_____
other _____	_____	_____

2. Find a classmate who is from a different country than you. Ask that person to be your partner. You will interview each other and try to find out all of the ways in which the capital city of your partner's country differs from that of your own country. You can add categories to the list below, and then fill in the contrasting details. Keep this information because you will need it for a later exercise.

Category	Partner's city	My city
size	_____	_____
climate	_____	_____
location in country	_____	_____

Category	Partner's city	My city
geography	_____	_____
night life	_____	_____
cultural attractions	_____	_____
transportation	_____	_____
pollution	_____	_____
other _____	_____	_____
other _____	_____	_____
other _____	_____	_____
other _____	_____	_____

THE TOPIC SENTENCE

Introduction

The topic sentence of the contrast paragraph is similar to that of a comparison paragraph. It names both of the topics that you will contrast and tells the reader that your paragraph will discuss their differences. You can begin your topic sentence with a general statement about the two subjects before you write your controlling idea (differences). That general statement is frequently a dependent clause or a prepositional phrase. The controlling idea should be presented in the main clause. The paragraph at the beginning of this chapter, for instance, begins with the general statement that Ron and Steve are brothers before it gives the controlling idea. This introductory statement makes the topic sentence more interesting. Normally you would expect brothers to have more similarities than differences, so when the author writes, "they have almost nothing in common," the topic sentence surprises you and catches your attention. You will practice writing introductory statements in some of the exercises in this chapter.

The same three rules apply to topic sentences, whether you are writing comparison or contrast paragraphs:

- Focus your topic, if necessary, by stating the aspects that will be contrasted.

- Mention both topics.

- Inform your reader that the paragraph will describe a contrast.

- Do not include more than one controlling idea.

Exercise 4.4 Look at the following topic sentence errors. With a partner (or as a class) rewrite each of the topic sentences correctly.

1. Canada is different from the United States in many ways. **(too general for one paragraph)**

   Make this topic sentence more specific.

   _____

2. Canada is different with respect to geography. **(only one topic is mentioned)**

   Write this topic sentence with two topics.

   _____

3. Canada and the United States are beautiful countries. **(not clear to reader that the paragraph will contrast the two countries)**

   Make this topic sentence introduce a **contrast.**

   _____

4. Canada and the United States have different landscapes for several reasons. **(mixes controlling ideas of "contrast" with "reasons")**

   Eliminate the extra controlling idea.

   _____

Sentence Patterns for Topic Sentences

The four topic sentence patterns below introduce the topics and the controlling idea for paragraphs of contrast. The patterns will help you write the "skeleton" of a good topic sentence for a paragraph of contrast. In the exercises that follow, you will write a general statement about each topic in a topic sentence. That statement will make your topic more interesting to the reader.

In the Chapter 4 Supplement, you will find more charts, examples, explanations, and exercises for each of the patterns.

Pattern #1

There are some amazing **differences between** Venus and Mercury.

Pattern #2
    a. Rhinos and hippos **are different** in three important ways.

    b. Coffee **is different from** tea in three important ways.

Pattern #3
    a. Dogs and wolves **are different with respect to** their physical appearance.

    b. Dogs **are different from** wolves **with respect to** their physical appearance.

Pattern #4
    a. The bobcat **differs from** the cougar in three ways.

    b. A bobcat **contrasts with** a cougar in three ways.

The general statement in the topic sentence frequently says something about the general topic or surprises the reader with a statement that you immediately contradict. It can be in a dependent clause or the first part of two sentences that are connected with *but* or *however*. Read the examples below. The *italicized* words are general statements about the topic.

They are members of the same species, but if you look closely, you can see that dogs and wolves are quite different with respect to their physical appearance. **(surprises the reader)**

Although it is difficult to see at first glance, dogs are different from wolves with respect to their physical appearance. **(makes reader curious)**

Although they are both planets in our solar system, there are some amazing differences between Venus and Mercury. **(general introduction to topic that surprises the reader)**

Exercise 4.5 Do this exercise with a partner. Use the patterns indicated to write topic sentences. Include an introductory statement for each of the topics. Refer to the Chapter 4 Supplement for more examples and explanations.

    1. television / radio

        Pattern #1: _____

        Pattern #2a: _____

        Pattern #2b: _____

        Pattern #3a: _____

        Pattern #3b: _____

        Pattern #4a: _____

        Pattern #4b: _____

2. Venezuela / Brazil

   Pattern #1: _____

   Pattern #2a: _____

   Pattern #2b: _____

   Pattern #3a: _____

   Pattern #3b: _____

   Pattern #4a: _____

   Pattern #4b: _____

3. socialism / capitalism

   Pattern #1: _____

   Pattern #2a: _____

   Pattern #2b: _____

   Pattern #3a: _____

   Pattern #3b: _____

   Pattern #4a: _____

   Pattern #4b: _____

4. German shepherds / poodles

   Pattern #1: _____

   Pattern #2a: _____

   Pattern #2b: _____

   Pattern #3a: _____

   Pattern #3b: _____

   Pattern #4a: _____

   Pattern #4b: _____

5. a dream / a nightmare

Pattern #1: _____

Pattern #2a: _____

Pattern #2b: _____

Pattern #3a: _____

Pattern #3b: _____

Pattern #4a: _____

Pattern #4b: _____

Exercise 4.6

Part 1

With a partner, list five possible topics for a contrast paragraph. Be sure that the topics you choose are interesting to both of you. You will use them for future writing assignments.

Example

_____differences between computer software and computer hardware_____

a. _____

b. _____

c. _____

d. _____

e. _____

Part 2

Write one topic sentence for each of the topics you chose. Use a different topic sentence pattern for each sentence. Add a general statement to each topic sentence.

a. _____

b. _____

c. _____

d. _____

e. _____

THE BODY OF THE CONTRAST PARAGRAPH

Introduction and Model Paragraph

Underline all of the words in the following paragraph that show contrast. Circle the transitional words and expressions.

There are some interesting differences between my two favorite teachers, Mrs. Jones and Mr. Smith. For example, they teach very different subjects. Unlike Mrs. Jones, who teaches chemistry and math, Mr. Smith teaches drama and music. These teachers also have different personalities. Mr. Smith is friendlier and more outgoing than Mrs. Jones. Mr. Smith likes to meet new people, but Mrs. Jones doesn't. Also, the two teachers have different hobbies. Mrs. Jones likes to study Japanese culture, and she collects old Japanese paintings and artifacts. She likes to stay home with her fascinating collection. In contrast, Mr. Smith prefers to play sports in his free time. He plays tennis and golf, and he hates to stay home. As you can see, Mr. Smith and Mrs. Jones seem completely different; however, both are great teachers and good friends.

In a contrast paragraph, organize the body of your paragraphs into three or more categories. The **categories** are nouns which tell your reader the aspect you are going to contrast, such as personality, height, price, or style. Write these categories in the main support sentences of your paragraph's body. Then give the details of the contrast in an additional sentence or two after the main support (this is called the **secondary support**).

In the previous chapter, you learned the difference between a main category and secondary support. In your comparison paragraph, you learned to introduce each comparison by first presenting a category and then adding secondary support that explained the similarity more completely (see pages 63–65). Each of your main supporting ideas did two things:

1. It introduced the category.
2. It explained the similarity between the two topics.

The same method of development is good for contrast paragraphs. The difference between the two types of paragraphs is that the sentences in the body of your contrast paragraph will contain more information than those in your comparison paragraph. Each main supporting idea will do three things:

1. It will introduce the category.
2. It will give the characteristic of the first topic.
3. It will give the contrasting characteristic of the second topic.

Look at the examples of categories and contrasts below and then read the sample sentences on the right. The first of each paired sentences is a **main support** sentence. It introduces a new point of contrast. The second of each paired sentences gives the secondary support or contrast that explains both of the different aspects. Look at the *italicized* words in the sample sentences. They give the contrast.

Category	Contrast	Sample Sentences
Level of difficulty	The midterm was difficult. The final exam was easy.	The exams differed in their levels of difficulty. The midterm differed from the final in that the midterm was *difficult,* but the final exam was *easy.*
Operating systems	The IBM runs DOS or OS2. The Macintosh runs its own operating system.	The computers have different operating systems. The IBM *runs* operating systems such as DOS or OS2, but the Macintosh *runs its own* proprietary operating system.
Level of intelligence	Tom is a child prodigy. Mark has a normal I.Q.	The boys have different levels of intelligence. Tom is a child *prodigy,* while Mark has a *normal* I.Q.
Height	My mother is tall. My father is short.	Another difference is their height. Although my mother is *tall,* my father is quite *short.*
Speed	The Porsche can go very fast. The Volkswagen Beetle doesn't go very fast.	As far as speed is concerned, the cars differ greatly. Unlike the Porsche, which can go very *fast,* the Volkswagen Beetle is a *slow* car.
Geographic location	San Francisco is by an ocean. Stockton is in a valley.	Another difference between San Francisco and Stockton is their geographic location. San Francisco is by an *ocean;* however, Stockton is in a *valley.*

Transitional Expressions for the Paragraph Body

Transitional expressions will help your reader see where one idea in your paragraph ends and another new idea begins. You should use them in all of your paragraphs of comparison and contrast. The transition sentence usually tells your reader about the next point of contrast (category). In the sentences below, the **category** words are highlighted. Read each sentence aloud with a classmate, paying attention to the *italicized* transitional expressions and categories.

Ask your partner: Is the point of the secondary support easier to understand when a transitional expression is included?

● Transitional Expressions for Category + First Supporting Detail

MAIN SUPPORT (CATEGORY)   SECONDARY SUPPORT

*…One important difference is that the tests had **different levels of difficulty**.* The midterm was very easy for most of the students in the class, but the final was so difficult that no student could pass it.

MAIN SUPPORT (CATEGORY)

*…For example, the IBM differs from the Macintosh with respect to the **operating systems they use**.* The IBM runs on DOS or OS2, while the Macintosh has its own special operating system and refers to that system with numbers such as "System 7."
SECONDARY SUPPORT

● Transitional Expressions for Category + Second or Third Supporting Detail

MAIN SUPPORT (CATEGORY)   SECONDARY SUPPORT

*…Tom and Mark also have different levels of **intelligence**.* Tom is a child prodigy; however, Mark has a normal I.Q.

MAIN SUPPORT (CATEGORY)   SECONDARY SUPPORT

*…Another difference between my mother and my father is their **height**.* Unlike my mother, who is tall, my father is rather short.

MAIN SUPPORT (CATEGORY)

*…Yet another difference between San Francisco and Stockton is their **geographic location**.* San Francisco is on an ocean; Stockton, on the other hand, is in a valley.
SECONDARY SUPPORT

• Transitional Expressions for Category + Last Supporting Detail

| MAIN SUPPORT (CATEGORY) | SECONDARY SUPPORT |

*...Finally, as far as **speed** is concerned, the two cars differ greatly.* The Porsche can go much faster than the Volkswagen.

Exercise 4.7 Look at the following pictures. With a partner, use the patterns above as models and write pairs of sentences for three pairs of pictures. The first of each pair will have a transition word and the name of an appropriate category. The second of each pair will name both of the topics and give a complete contrast.

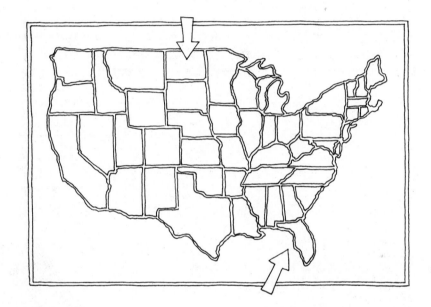

Example

...Another difference between North Dakota and Florida is the weather.

Unlike North Dakota, which has a bitterly cold winter, Florida has warm weather

all year round.

1.

desert   **tropical island**

_____

_____

_____

_____

2.

elm tree   **Christmas tree**

_____

_____

_____

_____

3.

personal computer   **laptop computer**

_____

_____

_____

_____

4.

lizard   **bird**

_____

_____

_____

_____

5.

John's eyes   **Steve's eyes**

_____

_____

_____

_____

In the next section of this chapter you will learn several sentence patterns that you can use to develop each supporting idea, or category, in your paragraph.

Sentence Patterns

● Introducing the Main Support: The Point of the Contrast

These two patterns will allow you to present the reader with the aspect that you are going to contrast.

Pattern #1

    a. Furthermore, John is **different from** Tony **with respect** to personality.

    b. Furthermore, John **contrasts with** Tony **in regard** to personality.

    c. Furthermore, John **differs from** Tony **with respect** to personality.

Pattern #2

My best friends, Tom and Mark, also **have** very **different** lifestyles.

Exercise 4.8   Do this exercise with a partner. Discuss each of the topics and write sentences using the topics and sentence patterns indicated. See the Chapter 4 Supplement for help.

1. Mary / Susan / height

   Pattern #1a: _____

   Pattern #1b: _____

   Pattern #1c: _____

2. Severino / Harold / cultural background

   Pattern #1a: _____

   Pattern #1b: _____

   Pattern #1c: _____

3. Nell / Walter / native language

   Pattern #2: _____

4. Miami / Atlanta / architectural styles

   Pattern #2: _____

• Introducing the Secondary Support: The Contrast Itself

These sentence patterns are used for the contrast itself. Use them after the transitional clauses that announce the category.

Pattern #1

Unlike my partner, **who** enjoys skiing and surfing during her vacations, **I** like to travel to foreign countries and go to concerts.

Pattern #2

Henry is popular, **while** Sam is hated by everyone.
While Henry is popular, Sam is hated by everyone.

Henry is popular, **whereas** Sam is hated by everyone.
Whereas Henry is popular, Sam is hated by everyone.

Pattern #3

Tom Cruise is **different from** Charles Bronson **in that** Mr. Cruise is quite popular among teenagers, but Mr. Bronson appeals more to the older generation.

Pattern #4

a. Tom likes chocolate ice cream; **however,** Steven prefers vanilla.

b. Tom likes chocolate ice cream. **In contrast,** Steven prefers vanilla.

c. Tom likes chocolate ice cream. Steven, **on the other hand,** prefers vanilla.

Pattern #5

a. Hurricanes are predictable, **but** earthquakes are not.

b. Hurricanes are predictable, **yet** earthquakes are not.

Pattern #6

a. Marsha was **taller than** Lucy.

b. Marsha was not **more serious than** Lucy.

c. Marsha had **a better** grade point average **than** Lucy.

d. Marsha owned **a more expensive car than** Lucy.

Exercise 4.9   Do this exercise with a partner. Discuss each of the topics and write sentences using the topics and sentence patterns as indicated. (In the Chapter 4 Supplement, you will find more charts, explanations, examples, and exercises for each of the patterns.)

1. the leader of my country / the leader of my partner's country (give the actual names of the two leaders in your sentences)

   Pattern #1: _____

   Pattern #2a: _____

   Pattern #2b: _____

   Pattern #3: _____

   Pattern #4a: _____

2. traveling by bus / traveling by airplane

   Pattern #3: _____

3. my partner's best friend / my best friend (give the actual names of the "best friends")

Pattern #4a: _____

Pattern #4b: _____

Pattern #4c: _____

4. your favorite aunt / your partner's favorite aunt

Pattern #5a: _____

Pattern #5b: _____

5. your favorite actor / your partner's favorite actor (give the actual names of the "favorite actors")

Pattern #6a: _____

Pattern #6b: _____

Pattern #6c: _____

Pattern #6d: _____

Exercise 4.10   Take the information you collected from the interview you did for Exercise 4.3. Write that information in the form of a paragraph on your own paper. Limit the support to three main topics. Use the sentence patterns you have learned in this chapter to write the topic sentence and body of the paragraph. Be sure to use transitional words and expressions to move from one main supporting idea to another.

THE CONCLUSION

The conclusion of your contrast paragraph must make the paragraph sound finished. It should make your reason for writing the contrast clear to your reader. In the concluding sentence, it is common to repeat the names of the two topics and then to offer an opinion, some advice, or an invitation to your reader.

Superlative Adjectives

When your purpose in a contrast paragraph is to show that one thing is better than another, the conclusion frequently uses a superlative adjective. You can read a more complete explanation of the superlative form of adjectives, with explanations, examples, and exercises in the Chapter 4 Supplement.

Lucky Marsha!

Marsha was **the sweetest** of all the girls.
Marsha was **the most intelligent** student in the class.
Marsha had **the wealthiest parents** of all.
Marsha learned **the most complicated** lessons with ease.

Exercise 4.11 Use the sentence patterns you have learned for comparatives and superlatives. Contrast the following pictures in two sentences. Use comparatives in the first sentence, and use a superlative in the second.

Example

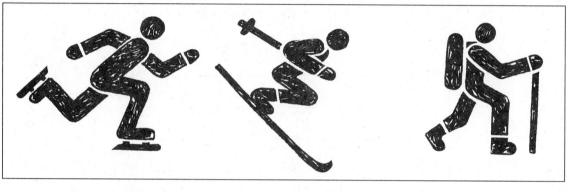

skating   skiing   hiking

a. Skiing is more exciting than skating.

b. Hiking is the most entertaining of all.

1.

a. _____

b. _____

2.

mouse   squirrel   rabbit

a. _____

b. _____

3.

bus   plane   ship

a. _____

b. _____

Exercise 4.12 Take two paragraphs from your work in this chapter (your own, the book's, or a classmate's) and write two different conclusions for each one. Copy (or photocopy) each paragraph once, and add the two conclusions below each copy.

Exercise 4.13 If possible, sit with the partner who helped you write the pattern sentences in Exercise 4.5 of this chapter. Plan and write a paragraph on your own paper using the information from ONE of the five topics. Use a concept map for your plan. Use transitional words and expressions in the body of the paragraph, and use the sentence patterns you have learned in this chapter.

Exercise 4.14 Take the information you collected from the interview you had with "a very different classmate" in Exercise 4.3. Write that information in the form of a paragraph. Limit the support to three main topics (choose the ones you like the best or group similar items under one category). Use the sentence patterns you have learned in this chapter to write the topic sentence and body of the paragraph. Be sure to use transitional words and expressions to move from one main supporting idea to another.

Exercise 4.15 With a partner (or alone if you prefer), write a paragraph based on the concept map below. Use all of the sentence patterns and transition words you have learned to develop a good topic sentence and body for your paragraph.

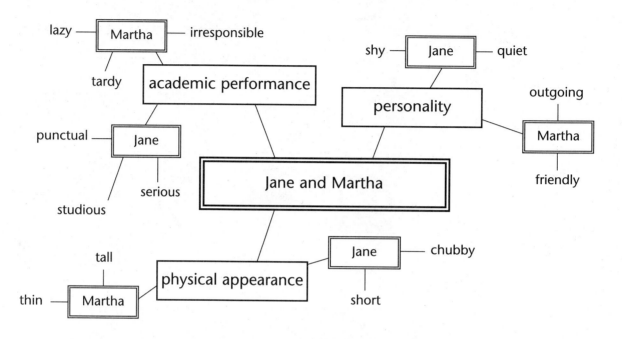

Exercise 4.16 Sit with a classmate for this exercise (if you want).

1. What is missing from the following paragraph? (Look at the concept map below for help.)

2. Add what is missing and rewrite the paragraph.

3. Write a conclusion for this paragraph.

There are important differences between a good student and a bad student. First, their attitudes in class are totally opposite. For example, the good student, who tries to be responsible and courteous in class, loves learning new ideas and sharing knowledge with classmates. Another difference is that the two types of students usually have different educational goals. Unlike the bad student, the good student knows why he or she is studying and is planning for a career, and this motivates him or her to study seriously. The good student also differs from the student with respect to ethical behavior in class. The bad student sometimes cheats on exams, plagiarizes writing, or copies exercises from other students in class.

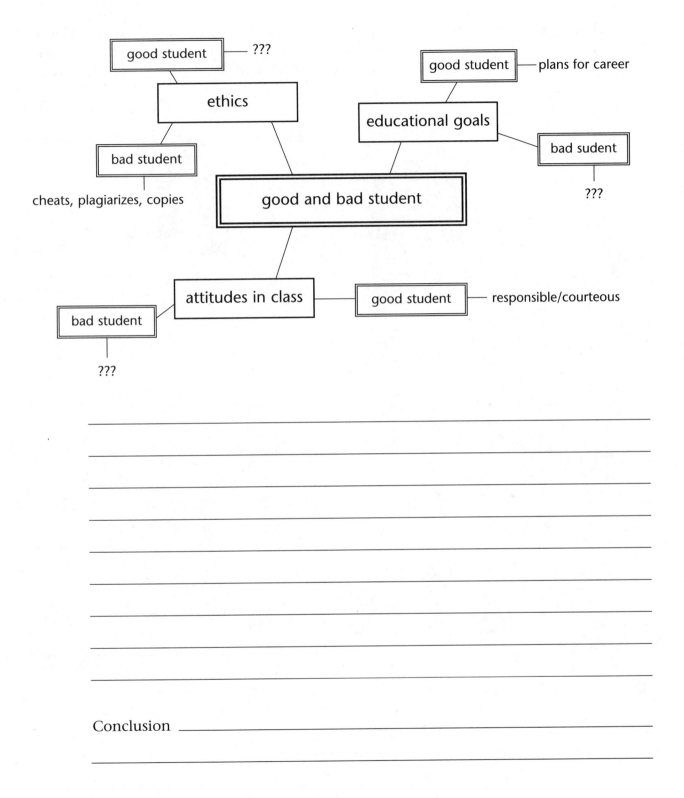

Conclusion _____

_____

Exercise 4.17 Write a contrast paragraph for ONE of the three pairs of animals below. Before you begin writing, plan your paragraph using a concept map or a list. Use the sentence patterns you have learned in this chapter for each part of your paragraph.

1.

_____

_____

_____

_____

_____

2.

_____

_____

_____

_____

_____

3.

_____

_____

_____

_____

_____

EDITING SYMBOLS

Problems with Sentences: Grammar and Syntax (*vt, shift, ^*)

- ## Verb Tense

Symbol	Meaning	Explanation
vt	Verb tense	The verb tense is wrong.

Examples

    Wrong: When you **will** arrive, we can leave.
                    vt
  Correction: When you arrive, we can leave.

    Wrong: If you **won** the lottery, what **will** you do?
                   vt
  Correction: If you **win** the lottery, what **will** you do?

This symbol indicates that you have chosen the correct verb, but that you are using it in the wrong verb tense. Verb tense errors can happen if a writer does not know which verb tense to use in certain grammatical structures, for example, when students use the future tense in time clauses.

Exercise 4.18 With a partner, find and correct the *vt* errors in the following sentences:

1. You will need to go through Customs as soon as you will arrive in Montreal.

   _____

2. As you will learn English, you will feel more confident when you will go to stores and talk to native speakers.

   _____

3. If you will study this, you will know what a dependent clause is.

   _____

4. We are understanding this now, but yesterday we do not understand it very well.

   _____

5. I am thinking you are a nice person.

   _____

Exercise 4.19 Find three *verb tense errors* in the assignments that have been returned to you and analyze them as follows.

Example

Error: John comed late to class last week, so the teacher was angry.

***vt* problem:** I put an irregular verb in the wrong form of the past tense.

Rule: The past tense of "come" is "came."

Correction: John came late to class last week, so the teacher was angry.

• Shift

Symbol	Meaning	Explanation
shift	Shift	The pronoun, tense, or number is not consistent.

Examples

Wrong: **People** need love because **you** can't grow up without it.
shift

Correction: **People** need love because **they** can't grow up without it.

Wrong: **A person** needs to do **his or her** homework if **you** want to pass.
shift

Correction: **A person** needs to do **his or her** homework if **he or she** wants to pass.

or: **Students** need to do **their** homework if **they** want to pass.

Wrong: Fran Tarkenton **was** one of football's greatest quarterbacks. He **is** a New York Giant.
shift

Correction: Fran Tarkenton **was** one of football's greatest quarterbacks. He **was** a New York Giant.

Wrong: If I **could** go with you, I **will.**
shift

Correction: If I **could** go with you, I **would.**

Wrong: All crime victims should report the **crime** to the police.
shift

Correction: All crime victims should report the **crimes** to the police.

Exercise 4.20 Correct the *shift* errors in the following sentences.

1. If I were you, I will go with them.
   shift

   _____

2. You should go to the beach, and don't go to the park.
   shift

   _____

3. I thought you say he wasn't here.
   shift

   _____

4. We really need to clean up our environment. People are not concerned with the
                                                        shift
   quality of air or water in this country. We must begin to recycle, and people have
                                             shift   *shift*
   to stop dumping industrial waste into our rivers and streams.

   _____

5. The workers in that factory are not happy with their salary.
                                                        shift

   _____

6. Writers have to be aware of shifts in person because you can confuse your audience
                                                        shift
   if you change from "they" to "you" in the same sentence. One must reread
                                                            shift
   everything he writes.

   _____

Exercise 4.21   Find three *shift errors* in the assignments that have been returned to
you, and analyze them as follows.

Example

Error: ___People have to be careful if you want to drive in that part of town.___

***shift* problem:** ___I mixed "they" (people) and "you" in the same sentence.___

Rule: ___Don't change person in a writing assignment.___

Correction: ___People have to be careful if they drive in that section of town.___

• Omission

Symbol	Meaning	Explanation
^	Omission	A word or words have been omitted here.

Examples

      Wrong: I gave it him.
                  ^

    Correction: I gave it **to** him.

      Wrong: When you going to return to Peru?
                     ^

    Correction: When **are** you going to return to Peru?

When you see this symbol, it means you have omitted a word from your sentence.

Exercise 4.22 With a partner, correct the ^ errors in the following sentences.

1. When person needs go downtown, he or she can take bus or metrorail. They both
        ^   ^   ^   ^

   cost the same amount money. Personally, I like take the bus because I can see
                        ^   ^

   more the city.
       ^

   _____

   _____

   _____

2. Listen the news. Is very dangerous go out because a hurricane coming.
      ^   ^   ^   ^

   _____

   _____

3. A person who talks every day and friendly is considered outgoing.
                             ^

   _____

   _____

4. In morning we took car to garage for checkup. The car not working.
   ^   ^   ^   ^   ^

_____

_____

Exercise 4.23 Find three *omission errors* in the assignments that have been returned to you, and analyze them as follows.

Example

Error: _People have be careful if they want drive in that part of town after dark._

omission **problem:** _I omitted prepositions with some of my verbs._

Rule: _Some verbs ("have," "need") always have "to" after them when they are_

followed by another verb.

Correction: _People have to be careful if they want to drive in that part of town after dark._

Paragraphs of Classification

The computer programs that accompany the editing symbols in this chapter are called: **Chapter 5—Disk 5** and **Chapter 5—Disk 2.**

INTRODUCTION AND MODEL PARAGRAPH

You have learned to plan and write paragraphs using examples, comparisons, and contrasts. In this chapter, you will use these skills to write paragraphs of classification. In these paragraphs, you will categorize things, such as merchandise in stores, areas of your campus, or types of teachers, according to their differences. Then you will use one or more items from each category as examples to describe the similarities among the items in each category.

You will also learn how to write informal and formal outlines in order to help organize your ideas into categories and subcategories. You will use the sentence patterns and connecting words that you have already learned to write the sentences in your paragraph.

Below is a model classification paragraph. It categorizes teachers into three types, and then gives the similar characteristics of each type of teacher. Read the paragraph with a partner, and then do the exercises that follow.

TEACHERS

Almost every teacher falls into one of three categories: the "Good Teacher," the "Great Teacher," or the "Indifferent Teacher." The Good Teacher is a teacher who effectively communicates with the students. This teacher is knowledgeable in the subject matter of the course, is well organized, and is willing to experiment with different teaching methods to make sure the class is interesting and that most of the students understand the course material. The Good Teacher gives several types of evaluations in a course and grades all students fairly. The second type of teacher, the Great Teacher, does all of this and more. The Great Teacher is an inspiration. This teacher's courses are exciting because he or she makes the class relevant to the students' lives. Each student in the Great Teacher's class feels like an important part of a dynamic group. This teacher learns from the students in the class and lets the class know that they have important contributions to make. In a Great Teacher's class, the student grows personally and academically. Unfortunately, there is another common type of teacher in schools: the Indifferent Teacher. Teachers who fall into this category have chosen the wrong profession, and they are easy to recognize. Indifferent Teachers do not try to learn the names of the students, always teach from the same text, and are unwilling to try new teaching techniques. They give the same exams, which are usually multiple-choice, every semester. The Indifferent Teachers do most or all of the talking in class and do not allow students to interact with them or with each other. In the Indifferent Teacher's class, everyone, including the teacher, frequently checks the clock because the time in class seems to drag.

Exercise 5.1 Discuss with a classmate: Have you ever had a "Great Teacher"? How has that teacher influenced you?

Exercise 5.2 Sit with a classmate, and discuss and answer these questions about the paragraph above.

1. What is the purpose of the topic sentence?

   _____

2. What are the focused topic and the controlling idea in the topic sentence?

   _____

3. How many categories of teachers are presented in the paragraph?

   _____

4. Do you agree with the author?

   _____

5. Does this paragraph sound finished? Does it have a concluding sentence?

   _____

6. What kinds of conclusions could you write for this paragraph?

   _____

7. Write a conclusion to this paragraph.

   _____

PLANNING AND DEVELOPING THE PARAGRAPH

You use classification every day. When you need to find an item in a department store, you look in the particular department where the item belongs. Because stores classify and store their merchandise in logical areas, it is usually easy to find what you are looking for. Can you imagine what a department store would be like if there were no departments? What would you do if the shoes, clothes, paint, toys, electronics, medicine, school supplies, jewelry, and books were all mixed together on the shelves? What if all the different kinds of clothing (children's, women's, men's, boys', and girls' clothes) were all together on the racks in the same area? As a shopper, you would feel frustrated trying to find what you need.

This same frustration happens when a reader tries to follow a badly organized paragraph. In searching for the point of the writing, the reader can get lost if he or she has to sort out the details and browse through unnecessary points. In writing individual paragraphs or essays, you can use **classification** to organize your ideas in a clear and logical pattern that your reader will easily understand.

Below is a diagram of a small neighborhood grocery store. The store owner has put similar items together on the shelves. Each section of the diagram is labeled according to the kind of merchandise it contains. For example, there is a **soda** section, a **bread** section, a **canned food** section, and a **book** section. Each of the sections contains similar items. The canned food section, for instance, has canned vegetables, canned fruit, canned meat, and canned pasta. There are different kinds of food in this section, but all of the products are similar in that they are all in cans.

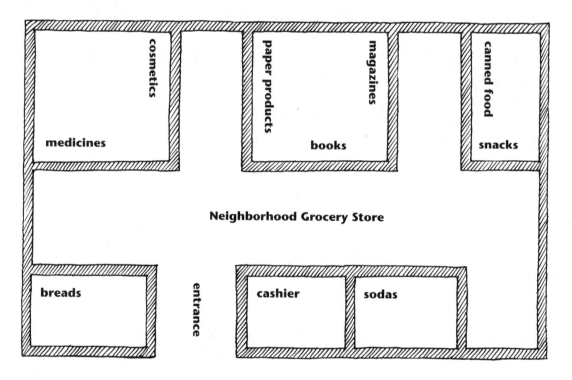

Exercise 5.3 (Class Activity) Discuss the following questions with a partner, and then do the six-step activity below together.

1. Why did the owner of this grocery store organize the merchandise in groups?

2. Within each section of a grocery store, are the items grouped in any special way (subcategories)?

Now use the diagram above to develop a classification paragraph. Follow each of the following steps carefully.

Step 1 (Think of the audience and purpose.)

Sit with a partner and look at the diagram of the neighborhood grocery store. The topic sentence for this paragraph will be:

> The Neighborhood Grocery Store would serve as a good organizational model for our own store.

This topic sentence tells the audience that your paragraph will discuss the organization of the Neighborhood Grocery Store, and that it will recommend using the same style of organization for "our own store." Who is the author of this paragraph? Who would be the audience for this paragraph? What is the purpose of a paragraph like this?

Step 2 (Brainstorm for details.)

List some of the subcategories (and examples of the items) that you might find in the different areas of the store:

Example

canned food section:

canned vegetables (corn, beets), canned meat (Vienna sausages, ham), canned pasta (spaghetti, macaroni)

1. book section:

   _____

   _____

2. soda section:

   _____

   _____

3. medicine section:

   _____

   _____

4. cosmetics section:

   _____

   _____

5. paper product section:

_____

_____

6. snack section:

_____

_____

● Step 3 (Develop ideas into sentences.)

Using a few of the examples from above, write two or three sentences to explain the similar characteristics of each of the following groups. Notice the use of passive voice in the sentences. (If you need to review the passive voice, see the Chapter 5 Supplement.) Use the example as a model sentence.

Example

sodas:

In the soda section, all of the beverages such as Pepsi, Coke, club soda, and ginger ale are stacked according to flavors. All of the products in the soda section are canned or bottled, and all are nonalcoholic.

1. cosmetics: _____

_____

_____

2. paper products: _____

_____

_____

3. snacks: _____

_____

_____

4. canned foods: _____

_____

_____

Step 4 (Write the first draft.)

Write the paragraph with your partner, using the topic sentence from Step 1 and some of the sentences you developed in Step 3. When you finish, write a conclusion for the paragraph. The conclusion can be an invitation, an opinion, or some advice.

Step 5 (Do a peer edit.)

Exchange paragraphs with another pair of students in the class. Read their paragraph and discuss with your own partner how their paragraph is different from your own.

Is their paragraph well organized?

Do you understand it?

Do you like their conclusion?   Why or why not?

Return the paragraphs, and tell the authors what you thought about their work.

Step 6 (Revise and turn in.)

With your partner, discuss what (if anything) you want to change about your paragraph based on the comments your classmates had. Revise your work, and turn it in.

Exercise 5.4   The following eight-step exercise will take you through the planning, organizing, and developing steps of writing a classification paragraph. All of the students in the class will have the same topic for this paragraph, but you will work in pairs or small groups and develop your own topic sentences. You will use everything you have learned in the previous chapters to do this exercise. First read the model paragraph below.

Students in this semester's writing class are different in many ways (language, culture, age), but one of the most fascinating differences is the variety of religious beliefs they hold. The students in the class can be divided into five religious groups. The first group, the Buddhists, include Kim, Lee, and, Cheng. These students believe in meditation and in the observance of moral truths. The second group is Christian: José, Marie, Anna, and Jenny. They follow the teachings of Jesus Christ, whom they believe to be the Son of God and the Savior of mankind. Next, we have three adherents of Islam: Muhammad, Gem, and Magda. Islam, which is the dominant religion in Asia, teaches that the Koran, their holy book, is the revelation of God to Muhammad. The Taoists in the class include Chuang and Hui Ming. Taoism is the principal philosophy and religion of China. It describes man's ideal state as freedom from desire. Lastly, we have three agnostics in the class who, although they do not deny the existence of God, believe that this existence cannot be logically proved (or disproved). These students are Carlos, Jean Paul, and Cornelius. There are many different religions in the world today, and with such a variety of cultural and religious beliefs represented in our class this semester, the students can expect to have a true multicultural experience.

● Step 1 Brainstorm and write the topic sentence.

Sit with a partner and look at the students in your classroom. How could you categorize all of the students in your classroom?

List five possible categories that would serve to divide the students in the room into groups. Then decide on ONLY ONE of those categories, and write a topic sentence for it. This category will be the basis for your classifications. Underline the category in your topic sentence and show it to your teacher. If your teacher approves of the topic sentence, write it on the chalkboard. The topic sentence in the paragraph above can serve as a model for your topic sentence.

● Step 2 Choose the topic sentence.

Look at all of the sentences on the board. Choose the one that you and your partner like the best. That will be the **topic sentence** for your paragraph. If you still like YOUR topic sentence the best, you should use it.

At this point you may need to take some time to interview students that you do not know in order to see where they might fit in your classification. If this is so, ask your teacher for "research time," and interview your classmates.

● Step 3 Plan the support.

On a separate piece of paper, put all the students in the class into categories. (Skip several lines after each category to have room for the details in Step 4.) Make sure to include all of the students in the class. You might have to expand the categories to do this.

Example

The author of the sample paragraph selected "religions" as the characteristic and grouped the students like this:

Religions
Buddhists: Kim, Lee, Cheng, Phuong
Christians: José, Marie, Anna, Jenny

Step 4 Expand the support.

For each of the categories you have listed in Step 3, write at least two similarities that the members of the category share. You might want to interview some of your classmates again for these additional details.

Example

Buddhists: Kim, Lee, Cheng, Phuong

>   All believe in a religion that teaches the practice of meditation and observance of moral truths.

Christians: José, Marie, Anna, Jenny

>   All follow the teachings of Jesus Christ, whom they all believe to be the Son of God and the Savior of mankind.

Step 5 Write the first draft.

With your partner, write a paragraph using the topic sentence you chose in Step 2 above. Use the details you wrote in Steps 3 and 4 above for the support of your paragraph. Do not write a conclusion yet.

Step 6 Do a peer edit.

Exchange paragraphs with another group. Write a conclusion for the other students' paragraph. The conclusion can be any style that you have learned in the previous chapters, but it must conclude the paragraph logically.

Step 7 Discuss and conclude.

Return all papers to the authors, and discuss the paragraph's conclusion with your partner. Edit if you want.

Step 8 Share.

If the instructor approves, volunteer to read your paragraph to the class.

Classification Paragraph Checklist

___ 1. I wrote a topic sentence for a specific audience and purpose.

___ 2. I planned the support carefully (outline).

___ 3. I developed compound and complex sentences for the body of the paragraph.

___ 4. I wrote the first draft.

___ 5. I proofread the draft or had a classmate read it.

___ 6. I revised and wrote the final draft.

CLASSIFICATION AND STEREOTYPING

Choosing the right **grouping** system is important. You can tell a lot about an author by the way that author classifies things, and some systems of classification can be wrong or unfair. Some systems of classifying people, for example, lead to **stereotyping:** putting people into groups and then assuming that all the people in a group are identical.

Exercise 5.5 Discuss one of the following scenarios with a partner, in small groups, or as a class:

Scenario 1

How might a racist person classify the population of this town if he/she were addressing a secret meeting of the Ku Klux Klan? What might be the author's purpose for this classification strategy? To instill brotherly love? (Does racism exist in your own countries?)

Scenario 2

How might a local politician who is seeking reelection classify the population of a city? What would be a possible purpose for this classification?

Scenario 3

How might a dictator classify the population of his/her nation to the generals of his army? What would be a possible purpose for this classification?

Think about this! How would a different audience affect each author's (above) method of classification? For example, what if the local politician had to address a group of high school students? Do you think the politician would tell the high school students that their concerns do not matter to him/her because students do not vote? Would the racist Ku Klux Klan member use the same classification system if he/she were a political candidate in a multicultural city?

Exercise 5.6 (Class Activity) Do this six-step exercise in pairs or small groups.

Step 1

Go to a busy location on your campus: library, cafeteria, bookstore, gymnasium, quad, or computer lab. Look around the area and decide what aspects of the location or the people there could be used to write a paragraph of classification.

Step 2

Discuss why you feel the categories you selected are appropriate. (For example, in the gymnasium, you may have divided the basketball players from the aerobics class because they were involved in such different activities.)

Step 3

Write down your categories and the reason for categorizing the area the way you did.

Step 4

Look at each category and list the similarities among the members of that group.

Step 5

Return to class and write a paragraph of classification based on your notes.

Step 6

If your instructor agrees, share your paragraph with the class.

PLANNING AND ORGANIZING THE SUPPORT (OUTLINING)

An outline for the body of the model paragraph at the beginning of this chapter might look like this:

I. The Good Teacher
   - A. Communication
   - B. Knowledge of subject matter
   - C. Organization
   - D. Teaching methods
   - E. Testing methods

II. The Great Teacher
   - A. Inspiration
   - B. Course relevance
   - C. Student participation in classes
   - D. Open-mindedness

III. The Indifferent Teacher
   A. Indifference toward students
   B. Course materials
   C. Classroom management
   D. Classroom atmosphere

An outline can help you plan and organize the points you want to present in a paragraph, an essay, or a longer writing assignment before you start the actual writing. When you write an outline, you divide your ideas into several main divisions and then list the subdivisions (details) under each main division. The outline can help you plan the structure of your paper, and it can help you see where you need to add main ideas or more details.

Informal Outlines

Unfortunately, starting to write by developing a formal outline first sometimes stops the flow of ideas. Formal outlines have a rigid structure, and if you have to concentrate on the structure of the outline instead of the content, writing can become very difficult. If this happens to you, you should use an informal outline (or list) to begin planning your paragraph, and then prepare a more formal outline after you add all of your details to your informal outline.

In an informal outline, you can use different types of sentences, and you do not need to worry about punctuation or capitalization of words. It might look like this:

1. ....
   A. ....

2. ....
   A. ....
   B. ....
   C. ....

3. ....
   A. ....
   B. ....

Formal Outlines

A formal outline has specific guidelines and punctuation rules, and can look like this:

```
I. .......
    A. .......
        1. ........
            a. .........
            b. .........
        2. .......
    B. .......
II. .......
III. .......
```

● Rules for Formal Outlines

Rule #1. The outline must be logical and clear. Each main division (I., II., III.,…) must be equally important points in the paragraph, represent the same level of classification as the previous main division, and be written with the same grammatical structure.

Wrong!	Correct!	Problem
I. Good teachers	I. Good teachers	"Great teachers" was not a
A. Great teachers	II. Great teachers	logical subdivision of "good
B. Indifferent teachers	III. Indifferent teachers	teachers."

Rule #2. The first letter of each entry in a formal outline is capitalized.

Wrong!	Correct!	Problem
I. good teachers	I. Good teachers	The headings were not
II. great teachers	II. Great teachers	capitalized.
III. indifferent teachers	III. Indifferent teachers	

Rule #3. Major headings and subheadings must be numbered (or lettered) and indented.

Wrong!	Correct!	Problem
I. Good teachers	I. Good teachers	The subheadings were not
Learn names of students	A. Learn names of students	numbered or indented.
Grade exams fairly	B. Use different teaching methods	
II. Great teachers	II. Great teachers	

Rule #4. Every heading must have a "partner." For every "I," there must be a "II." For every "A," there must be a "B." If you have only a single subheading, incorporate it into the main heading above it.

Wrong!

I. Good teachers
   A. Learn names of students
II. Great teachers

Correct!

I. Good teachers
   A. Learn names of students
   B. Use different teaching methods
II. Great teachers

Problem

There was no "B" for the "A."

Rule #5. Don't mix outline styles. There are two styles of formal outlines that you can use for paragraphs: a topic outline, which uses noun phrases for each heading, or a sentence outline, which uses a complete sentence for each heading. Ask your own instructor which style of outline you should write in this class.

Wrong!

I. Good teachers
II. Great teachers are hard to find
III. Indifferent teachers

Correct!

I. Good teachers
II. Great teachers
III. Indifferent teachers

Problem

The outline mixed topics with sentences in the headings.

Exercise 5.7 Create outlines on your own paper for two of the paragraphs you have written in this chapter (or in the book).

Exercise 5.8 (Audience and Purpose) In this exercise, you will develop an outline for a classification paragraph for a classmate (audience). You will write a paragraph based on your classmate's outline, and he or she will write a paragraph based on yours. Because the audience for your outline is somebody else, it is important to make your outline clear, logical, and complete.

Step 1 (Brainstorm for a topic.)

Decide which characteristic should be used to categorize each of the following topics.

Example

a menu in a restaurant

   type of dish (hors d'oeuvres, entrée, etc.)

_____

1. a state

_____

2. a doctor's office

_____

3. your country

_____

4. popular singers

_____

5. music

_____

6. students

_____

7. this city

_____

8. cities in this country

_____

9. hobbies

_____

Step 2 (Choose a topic and write an informal outline.)

Select one of the above topics, and plan a paragraph with an **informal outline.**

Step 3 (Share and revise.)

Show your outline to a classmate. If he or she does not understand your outline, take it back and revise it.

Step 4 (Write a formal outline.)

Take your outline back and develop a **formal outline** for the paragraph.

Step 5 (Trade outlines and write the paragraph.)

Exchange outlines with a classmate. Write a paragraph of classification using the "borrowed" outline.

Step 6 (Share.)

Let your classmate read your paragraph. Ask if your paragraph is what he/she expected.

Step 7 (Listen and revise.)

Listen to your classmate's comments. Revise the paragraph if you think you should.

Step 8 (Write final draft.)

Write the final draft of the paragraph and turn it in.

Exercise 5.9 (Optional Writing Project) Choose a stereotyping scenario from Exercise 5.5. Pretend to be the author of the scenario with the purpose and audience explained. Plan (outline) and write the paragraph that the scenario would produce. When you finish, give your own opinion about what you have written.

EDITING SYMBOLS

Problems with Words (sp, ww, wf)

• Spelling

Symbol	Meaning	Explanation
sp	Spelling	The word is not spelled correctly.

Examples

> **Wrong:** This isn't **rite.**
> > *sp*
> **Correction:** This isn't **right.**

Wrong: Is this **there** pen or **hour** pen?
    sp   sp
Correction: Is this **their** pen or **our** pen?

To correct your spelling problems, look the word up in the dictionary. (It helps to use your bilingual dictionary for this purpose.)

Exercise 5.10   Correct the *sp* errors in the following sentences:

1. She adviced me to check the ofice for the date of the apointment.
        sp   sp   sp

    _____

2. My neiborhood is not verry safe. I woud like to move.
        sp   sp   sp

    _____

3. The pares and aples are in aile 2 next to the peeches and graipefruit.
        sp   sp   sp   sp   sp

    _____

4. Don't exagerate. This wrod can't be speled rong. I just looked it up.
        sp   sp   sp   sp

    _____

Exercise 5.11   Find three **spelling errors** in the assignments which have been returned to you, and analyze them using the following chart. (Try to find words that you have spelled wrong more than one time.)

Example

Error   **Correction**

exagerate   exaggerate

Error   **Correction**

1. _____   _____

2. _____   _____

3. _____   _____

• **Wrong Word**

Symbol	Meaning	Explanation
ww	Wrong word	The word is not used correctly.

Examples

> **Wrong:** I **made** a test and got a good **note.**
> ⠀⠀⠀⠀⠀⠀⠀*ww*⠀⠀⠀⠀⠀⠀⠀⠀⠀⠀⠀⠀*ww*
> **Correction:** I **took** a test and got a good **grade.**

> **Wrong:** I **assist** class **all** days.
> ⠀⠀⠀⠀⠀⠀*ww*⠀⠀⠀⠀*ww*
> **Correction:** I **attend** class **every** day.

This symbol indicates that you have selected the wrong word. This happens frequently when you are learning a new language. The secret for choosing the correct word in a bilingual dictionary is first to look up the word in your own language, and then, after you think you have selected the appropriate English word from the options, look that English word up in the English section of your bilingual dictionary and see if the translation gives the meaning you are looking for.

Exercise 5.12 Correct the *ww* errors in the following sentences:

1. Sometimes when people take Pepsi and Coke they cannot feel the difference.
⠀⠀⠀⠀⠀⠀⠀⠀⠀⠀⠀*ww*⠀⠀⠀⠀⠀⠀⠀⠀⠀⠀⠀⠀⠀⠀⠀⠀⠀⠀*ww*

_____

2. I drove to their house to recollect them and carry them to school.
⠀⠀⠀⠀⠀⠀⠀⠀⠀⠀⠀⠀⠀⠀*ww*⠀⠀⠀⠀⠀⠀⠀⠀*ww*

_____

3. In the village, there were no electrical appliances because people didn't know about this knowledge.
⠀⠀⠀⠀⠀*ww*

_____

4. I do not like to assist reunions at work when the boss is out of town.
⠀⠀⠀⠀⠀⠀⠀⠀*ww*⠀⠀⠀*ww*

_____

5. I have many families, but I live along.
   ww   *ww*

   _____

6. Do you think than it will rain later?
   ww

   _____

7. I think to go to South America the proximate year.
   ww   *ww*

   _____

Exercise 5.13 Find three *wrong word errors* in the assignments that have been returned to you, and analyze them as follows. (Try to find words that you have spelled wrong more than one time.)

Error: ___I **made** my homework last week._____

Correction: ___I **did** my homework last week._____

Explanation: ___The teacher MAKES the test. "Make" means "to create." The student

DOES the homework. "Do" means "perform."_____

● Word Form

Symbol	Meaning	Explanation
wf	Word form	The word is written in the wrong form (adverb, adjective, noun).

Examples

      Wrong: Hank sings **good.**
                           wf
Correction: Hank sings **well.**

Wrong: We **use** to study German.
wf
Correction: We **used** to study German.

This symbol indicates that you have selected the right word, but have written the wrong form of the word in your sentence. Maybe you needed an adjective, but the word you wrote was an adverb or a noun.

Exercise 5.14   With a partner, find and correct the *wf* errors in the following sentences:

1. My car was damage by the storm. It affected me mental and physical.

2. My mother-in-law agreement with my mother that having a unite family is very important.

3. They have certainly physique characteristics in commonly.

4. For example, some countries allow to drink in the street.

5. Suddenly the car, which the driver couldn't control, slid off the roadside and hit a tree.

6. I have become more and more self-reliance.

7. She is getting used to live here.

8. Coke and Pepsi have the same brown colorful, and they producing a lot of bubbles that tingle in your throat when you drink them.

9. He came to class lately.

_____

10. We don't speak English very good yet, but we are learning quick.

_____

Exercise 5.15 Find three **word form errors** in the assignments which have been returned to you, and analyze them as follows.

Example

Error: Jane drives too quick.

word form problem: quick = quickly

Explanation: If the word describes an action, it must be an adverb. "Drive" is an action. "Quick" is an adjective.

Correction: Jane drives too quickly.

Problems with Logic *(logic)*

Symbol	Meaning	Explanation
(logic) (??)	Faulty logic or meaning unclear.	This part (word, sentence, section) is unclear.

Example

Wrong: Because I studied, I failed the test.
              ??
Correction: I didn't study, so I failed the test.

A logic problem in a paragraph happens when an idea is not explained fully or clearly, when an oversimplification or generalization is made, or when the order of ideas is confusing or unclear.

Exercise 5.16 Find and discuss the *logic* errors in the following paragraphs with a partner:

When foreign people come to other countries, they don't have any idea about the differences between their own country and the countries which they are visiting. It is sometimes better to know the differences than not to know them; however, when people plan to travel, they don't care about these little details. For example, some countries allow drinking at any age, but it is banned there. Foreign people could avoid many problems that always begin when they do not know the rules or lifestyle of the countries that they are visiting.

Drugs should be illegal because they can be dangerous for three reasons. First of all, drugs usually affect people mentally and physically; therefore, drug addicts almost always have accidents. In addition, drug addicts are people, so many of them can feel faint and destroy things. Finally, people can rarely have peace when they walk on the street because people who drive and walk are not fair, or they are not fine. I think drugs are very dangerous for our health.

chapter
six

Paragraphs of Definition

What is it?

The computer program that accompanies the editing symbols in this chapter is called: **Chapter 6—Disk 1**

INTRODUCTION AND MODEL PARAGRAPH

Read the model paragraph below, and answer the questions that follow.

Plagiarism means taking another person's words and using them as your own. In the United States, plagiarism is considered dishonest. In fact, it is considered a serious crime in much of the academic and professional world. Everyone knows that cheating on tests is wrong, but many do not realize that plagiarizing is a form of cheating. The consequences can be serious if a student is caught plagiarizing in a class. Every school has its own method of punishing plagiarists. In some schools, the student is asked to explain the motive (reason) for the offense. Then the student is put on probation for a period of time. At other schools, the student will receive an F on the assignment and get a second chance. In some schools, however, the plagiarist is expelled from class or from the school. The next time you use information from another person's writing, be sure to use quotation marks around the author's words or paraphrase the words, giving credit to the author for his or her ideas.

1. What kind of paragraph is this?

2. What is the topic of the paragraph?

3. What kind of support is used in the body of the paragraph?

4. What do you think about the content of this paragraph? Do you understand the idea of "plagiarism"? What are your country's policies on plagiarism?

What Is It?

Exercise 6.1 Sit with a partner. Read the following definitions and tell what "it" is.

1. **It** is a tall, woody plant with one trunk, many branches, and many leaves.

   _____

2. **It** is a fragrant liquid that is distilled from flowers. _____

3. **It** is a man who is not married. _____

4. **It** is a group of people who judge and give a verdict in court. _____

5. **It** is an inexpensive writing instrument consisting of a cylindrical piece of wood approximately six inches long with a graphite center and an eraser attached to the top. _____

TYPES OF DEFINITIONS

Introduction

From time to time in your academic courses, you will need to write a definition of a term. There are several kinds of definitions that you can use depending upon your audience and purpose. In this chapter, you will learn to write word substitution definitions, short formal definition sentences, extended definition paragraphs, and stipulated (or personal) definitions.

You will be able to use everything you have learned in the previous chapters when you write definition paragraphs because the type of support (method of development) for these paragraphs is flexible. You can use comparison-contrast, examples or details, enumeration, or a combination of these to define a term. This is why the definition paragraph is presented last in the textbook. It is more flexible than the others you have written up to this point. Enjoy this freedom, but don't abuse it. If you use too many unrelated styles of development in the body of any paragraph, you might confuse your audience as to the purpose of your paragraph.

The grammatical structures that are discussed in the Chapter 5 and Chapter 6 Supplements, the passive voice and adjective phrases, will both be used in the assignments for this chapter.

Word Substitution Definitions

The shortest definition you can write is called a "word substitution definition." It is written as a synonym (within parentheses) after the word. Use the word substitution definition only when you are sure your audience (your reader) will not understand the meaning of your words, and keep it short.

Examples

The salad was near the congrís (the Cuban black bean and rice dish).

Tom's mother definitely has a strong maternal (motherly) instinct. She has adopted eight children.

The difficult journey was not an impediment (obstacle) for Julio.

Hank's money was dwindling (disappearing), so he stopped gambling and went home.

Exercise 6.2 A word substitution definition is correct as long as the explanation is brief. A typical word substitution definition simply gives a common synonym (one word) for the term. The following sentences show three common errors to avoid when you write this kind of definition.

Error #1: Don't give a long definition inside the parentheses. Write only a one- or two-word synonym or a very short explanation. Correct this sentence.

Arepas (a typical Venezuelan food made of white corn meal patties that are fried, baked, or boiled and served at breakfast or dinner as a bread substitute or stuffed with fillings for a fast lunch) are delicious corncakes filled with tuna, cheese, or ham.

_____

_____

Error #2: Don't use a word inside parentheses that is more difficult to understand than the term you are defining. Correct the following sentence.

The rain (precipitation) was beating against the window.

_____

Error #3: Don't use too many word substitutions in a sentence (or paragraph). Correct the following sentence.

The disparaging (insulting) remark (comment) rankled (bothered and angered) Sharon, so she gave a stinging (hurtful) retort (answer) and fled the room (left the room quickly).

_____

_____

Exercise 6.3 With a classmate, write sentences using the following words. Use the synonym in parentheses as a word substitution definition in each sentence. The word may be a noun, verb, or adjective.

Example

garrulous (talkative)

Jonathan was not popular at family reunions because he was such a boring, garrulous (talkative) old man.

1. remuneration (payment)

_____

2. scrutinize (examine carefully)

_____

3. acerbity (bitterness)

_____

Short Formal Definitions

Another type of definition is the short "formal definition," which is a one-sentence dictionary-style definition. This definition explains the meaning of a term by describing the characteristics that distinguish it from other members of its *group*. You will use this type of definition when you need to write a very short concise definition, but you can also use it as your topic sentence for a definition paragraph.

Examples

TOPIC   CATEGORY
An everglade is a tract of marshy land covered mostly with tall grass and hammocks.
                  DISTINGUISHING CHARACTERISTICS

TOPIC   CATEGORY
A dog is a domesticated canine raised in a variety of breeds.
            DISTINGUISHING CHARACTERISTICS

The short formal definition consists of three parts:

1. The *thing* to be defined (the topic).

2. The *category* that the thing belongs to.

3. The *characteristics* that distinguish the thing from all of the other things in its category.

Examples

A ball is a small round rubber toy that bounces.
TOPIC   CATEGORY   DISTINGUISHING
              CHARACTERISTICS

An elephant is a large grey mammal with a long, flexible trunk.
  TOPIC   CATEGORY   DISTINGUISHING
              CHARACTERISTICS

Exercise 6.4   Do this exercise with a partner. In a monolingual (English-English) dictionary, look up the definitions for the following words. If the word has more than one form, choose the noun form for this exercise.   Write the one-sentence definition for each of the following nouns. Circle the category and underline the distinguishing characteristics in each sentence.

1. coral _____

_____

2. redwood _____

_____

3. February _____

_____

4. shackle _____

_____

5. shade _____

_____

6. cabbage _____

_____

● The Six-Step Process

The planning (or thought process) involved in writing the topic sentence for your definition involves six steps. You do not need to do all of the steps on paper when you write your topic sentence, but you do need to do them in your head.

Steps	Examples
Step #1. Choose a topic.	→ an **elephant**
Step #2. Name its category.	→ **mammal**
Step #3. Add some additional descriptive words to narrow the category, if possible.	→ **large** mammal **grey**

Step #4. Think of all the things that also fit into this category.	→	**rhinoceros** = large grey mammal **hippopotamus** = large grey mammal
Step #5. Determine how your topic is different from all the things that also fit into this category.		an elephant **has a trunk** (hippos and rhinos do not have trunks)
Step #6. Write the topic sentence with the topic, category, and distinguishing features.		**An elephant is a large grey mammal with a long, flexible trunk**

Exercise 6.5   In the following exercise, you will practice planning three topic sentences of definition with a partner. Look at the example ("mouse") and at the chart above for help with each step. Do not use an English-English dictionary for this exercise. However, if your instructor allows, you may use a bilingual dictionary.

Step #1   Sit with a partner for this exercise. List three nouns that would be interesting to define.

Example

mouse

1. _____

2. _____

3. _____

Step #2   List the category (class, group, species, etc.) that each of the three nouns from above belongs to.

Example

mouse = rodent

1. _____

2. _____

3. _____

Step #3 Now add some descriptive words to each category.

Example

mouse = rodent → *small grey* rodent

1. _____

2. _____

3. _____

Step #4 Now think of all of the other things in the world that would also fit into the three *categories* you have listed.

Example

mouse = rodent → small grey rodent → *so is a rat* and *a gopher*

1. _____

2. _____

3. _____

4. others: _____

Step #5 Now think of the characteristics that make your topic different from all of the other things listed in the *categories* above. (These will be the "distinguishing characteristics.")

Example

A mouse is smaller than a rat or a gopher, and it has floppy ears.

1. _____

2. _____

3. _____

Step #6 Now write a topic sentence for each of the definitions you have developed.

Example

A mouse is a small grey rodent which has floppy ears.

1. _____

2. _____

3. _____

Check your work with this planning checklist:

Planning Checklist: Topic Sentence for Formal Definition

___ 1. I chose a topic.

___ 2. I named the category that the topic belongs to.

___ 3. I added adjectives to the category to narrow it.

___ 4. I thought of other things that fit in the category.

___ 5. I determined how my topic differed from all the things that are in this category.

___ 6. I wrote a topic sentence with the topic, category, and distinguishing features.

A riddle is a question or statement that requires thought to answer or solve.

A fun way to check that your topic sentence is correct is to take out the topic (replace it with "it" or "they"), and make a riddle out of the sentence and read it to a classmate. If the only possible answer that your classmate can find to your riddle is the topic you have selected, then your topic sentence is good. If your classmate can think of several correct answers to your riddle, then you have not given very good "distinguishing characteristics."

Exercise 6.6 Practice with these riddles. Can you and your partner tell what the topic is in each of these sentences? Write the topic in the blank, and then circle the category and underline the distinguishing characteristics of each topic sentence. One of the sentences is bad because there are several possible answers to the riddle. Find it and correct it.

Example

A ___table___ is **a piece of furniture** *supported by vertical legs and having a flat horizontal surface.*

1. _____ is **a firearm** *designed to be used with only one hand.*

2. _____ is **the uppermost part of the body** *containing the brain, eyes, nose, mouth, and jaws.*

3. _____ is **a legless, scaly reptile** *with a long, tapering, cylindrical body.*

4. _____ is **a horse-like African mammal** *with black and white stripes.*

5. _____ is **a season** *of the year.*

Exercise 6.7 With your partner, take a piece of paper and write riddles for the three topic sentences you have developed. To do this, write your topic sentence, but omit the topic. When the class has finished, walk around to the other pairs of students in your classroom, read your riddles to them, and see if they can guess your topics. Then see if you and your partner can guess their topics. If your classmates can think of more than one topic that fits your riddle, then you must rewrite or expand your "distinguishing characteristics."

Exercise 6.8 Sit with a partner or in small groups and correct these topic sentences of definition. First discuss what is wrong with each topic sentence, then rewrite them.

1. A horse is an animal found on a farm.

   _____

2. Economics is the study of economy.

   _____

3. Lemonade is a cool, refreshing drink.

_____

4. Dogs are wonderful house pets.

_____

5. The dollar is an American currency.

_____

Extended Definitions

The extended definition is frequently used to give additional information about a term. This type of definition can begin with the short formal definition, but then it gives more information. The body of this type of paragraph can be developed using synonyms, examples, descriptions, comparison, contrast, and various other methods of development. If your topic is "horse," for example, you could describe the physical characteristics of the horse; you could write a classification paragraph about the different breeds of horses found in South America; you could compare or contrast two or more breeds of horse to define what a good "work horse" consists of; or you could narrate the horse's evolution. In most of the paragraphs you have studied in this text, you limited your support to one method of development. In the body of this kind of paragraph, the method of support you use is flexible, and you can use more than one method in one paragraph. In addition, definition paragraphs of this type sometimes do not need a conclusion.

Exercise 6.9 Read the following paragraph with a classmate, and discuss the questions that follow with a partner, in small groups, or with the class.

A telescope is a system of lenses which gathers and focuses light from objects in space too distant to see clearly with the naked eye. It forms a clear optical image of the distant object, allowing astronomers to study it in more depth. The telescope was invented in the 17th century. The invention of the telescope permitted early astronomers to measure the positions and motions of the planets and other celestial bodies, and also to study their physical composition. The most powerful telescopes are found in observatories located at high altitudes in unpopulated areas.

1. What kind of topic sentence does this paragraph have?

2. What method of support is used in the body of the paragraph? (narration? description? comparison? contrast? examples?)

3. How many adjective phrases can you find in the paragraph? (See the Chapter 7 Supplement to review adjective phrases.)

4. Does the paragraph have a conclusion?

5. Does the paragraph sound finished?

6. Where would you see a paragraph like this?

● Generating Ideas for the Extended Definition

To generate ideas for the body of a definition paragraph, you first need to determine your purpose and audience. Your purpose for writing the paragraph will determine the method or methods you use in the body of the paragraph. To determine your purpose, ask yourself the following questions:

Do I want to **narrate the history** of the thing I am defining?

Do I want to **compare** it to a similar *thing* and show that it is superior or inferior to that other *thing?*

Do I want to **describe** it?

Do I want to break it down into **categories** and describe each category?

Do I want to explain **how it works?**

Do I want to do several of these things in the same paragraph?

If you still do not know how you want to define your topic, you can ask yourself some specific questions like those below. As you write answers to the questions, you explore different aspects of your topic and will probably find one or more that interest you. This prewriting activity is called *freewriting*.

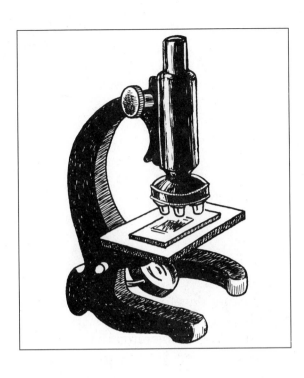

Microscope

What is it?

How does it work?

What is its history?

How many different kinds are there?

Is one brand better than the others? Why?

Giraffe

What is it?

What does it look like?

Why does it have such unique physical characteristics?

Where does it live?

What are its habits?

How has man affected this species' existence?

After you have determined the purpose of your paragraph, you must consider your audience. You want to select details, examples, a description, or an explanation that will interest your reader. Then you are ready to develop your paragraph. You can follow the process of writing that you learned in previous chapters:

Checklist for Paragraphs of Definition

  __   1. Freewrite to get ideas for the paragraph.

  __   2. Eliminate the unrelated ideas.

  __   3. Add more details to the ideas.

  __   4. Organize the ideas logically.

  __   5. Write the first draft.

  __   6. Proofread or peer edit.

  __   7. Edit and write the final draft.

Exercise 6.10   Using the three topics you and your partner developed in Exercise 6.5, follow the seven-step process above and write a paragraph for one of the topics. You will use the topic sentence you developed in Exercise 6.5. You might have edited that topic sentence in Exercise 6.7 if it was not clear to your classmates. If you did, use the new topic sentence.

Stipulated Definitions

You need to write an interpretation or clarification of a word if you feel your audience will not agree with your interpretation of it, or if you are going to use the word in an unexpected way. In these cases, you can use a "stipulated definition." In the stipulated definition, you explain your (or another person's) interpretation of a term, or you inform your reader that of several possible meanings of a term, you will use only one of the interpretations. The word or phrase that you define can be an abstract noun or a concrete noun that you are using in a nonstandard way.

● Personal Interpretations

In the following topic sentences, the author plans to (1) analyze another person's interpretation of a term, (2) give his or her own interpretation of a term, or (3) use a term in a nonstandard way. Can you tell which is which?

In the 1960s, the hippies in America had a unique concept of **success.**

Gabriel García Marquez's book, *One Hundred Years of Solitude,* presents the audience with a magical view of **reality.**

Love means different things to different people.

A person's concept of **wealth** changes with age.

The chairperson of the science department is a walking **computer.**

Exercise 6.11 Write topic sentences for three of the following abstract nouns. You may use patterns from any of the three types of sentences above.

1. wealth—defined by a capitalist
2. wealth—defined by a socialist
3. wealth—your own definition
4. success
5. a good politician
6. a good son/daughter
7. a good parent
8. the perfect date
9. the perfect world
10. the ideal spouse

1. _____

2. _____

3. _____

Clarifying Terms by Stipulated Definitions

When the author needs to explain that of all the possible meanings of a term, only one will be used, or to explain how a particular term is going to be used for a specific purpose (popular in legal documents), he or she can offer a clarification. The second two examples below are examples of how this type of definition is used in legal documents. You will not practice legal writing style here, but see if you can understand the sentences. Legal English is not easy to read.

Examples

The word "Venus" is used here to refer to the Roman goddess of love, and not the planet.

The term "atmosphere" is used here to refer to the feelings or ambiance in the room, and not the quality of the air in it.

Legal terminology

The persons listed in Article 1, number 1, of the American Investment Act, herein referred to as **the Client,** will be summoned to court within one month of the date of this action.

Henry Gomez, hereafter referred to as **The Party of the First Part,** resides in Atlanta, Georgia.

Exercise 6.12 Using the first two examples above, write a "clarification of terms" for two of the words below:

1. Paris (the capital city of France **or** the Greek who started the Trojan War)

   _____

2. accessory (something helpful but not essential **or** a person who helps

   commit a crime)

   _____

3. ideal (something imaginary **or** something perfect)

   _____

4. maid (an unmarried girl **or** a female servant)

   _____

Exercise 6.13 By yourself, with a partner, or in a small group you will write a definition paragraph which will explain how death is viewed by three different groups of people: existentialists, Buddhists, and Christians. To write this assignment, you should research the topic (in the library or with interviews). Outline your ideas before you write your paragraph, and turn in the outline with the assignment.

Topic: The meaning of death:

defined by an existentialist

defined by a Buddhist

defined by a Christian

Exercise 6.14 In Chapter 5, you saw the following paragraph of classification. The support consists of stipulated definitions for three types of teachers: the "Good Teacher," the "Great Teacher," and the "Indifferent Teacher." For this exercise, you may use the same structure to develop a paragraph about "types of students." You will be using classification and definition. If you want, you can limit the topic to one or two categories. Write a conclusion to your paragraph (this paragraph doesn't have one).

TEACHERS

Almost every teacher falls into one of three categories: the "Good Teacher," the "Great Teacher," and the "Indifferent Teacher." The Good Teacher is a teacher who effectively communicates with the students. This teacher is knowledgeable in the subject matter of the course, is well organized, and is willing to experiment with different teaching methods to make sure the class is interesting and that most of the students understand the course material. The Good Teacher gives several types of evaluations in a course and grades all students fairly. The second type of teacher, the Great Teacher, does all of this and more. The Great Teacher is an inspiration. This teacher's courses are exciting because he or she makes the class relevant to the students' lives. Each student in the Great Teacher's class feels like an important part of a dynamic group. This teacher learns from the students in the class and lets the class know that they have important contributions to make. In a Great Teacher's class, the student grows personally and academically. Unfortunately, there is another common type of teacher in schools: the Indifferent Teacher. Teachers who fall into this category have chosen the wrong profession, and they are easy to recognize. Indifferent Teachers do not try to learn the names of the students, always teach from the same text, and are unwilling to try new teaching techniques. They give the same exams, which are usually multiple-choice, every semester. The Indifferent Teachers do most or all of the talking in class and do not allow students to interact with them or with each other. In the Indifferent Teacher's class, everyone, including the teacher, frequently checks the clock because the time in class seems to drag.

EDITING SYMBOLS

Problems with Sentence Connecting (p, frag, ro, cs)

Punctuation

Symbol	Meaning	Explanation
p	Punctuation	The sentence has an error in punctuation.

Examples

Wrong: If it rains I will get wet.

Correction: If it rains, I will get wet.
$\quad\quad\quad\quad\quad\quad\quad\;p$

Wrong: I studied, however I failed.

Correction: I studied; however, I failed.
$\quad\quad\quad\quad\quad\quad\quad\;\;p\quad\quad\;\;p$

This symbol indicates an error in punctuation. (To review the basic rules of punctuation, as well as punctuation of subordinate clauses, coordinating conjunctions, and transitional words and expressions, refer to Appendix 2.)

Exercise 6.15 Correct the punctuation errors in the following sentences:

1. When the rain started *p* everyone ran into the house.
   (COMMA AFTER SUBORDINATE CLAUSE)

2. James Thomas *p* who teaches advanced speech classes *p* knows Judy Gilbert personally.
   (COMMAS AROUND APPOSITIVES)

3. Did you add the figures in column B first *p*
   (QUESTION MARK AT END OF INTERROGATIVE)

4. Shrubs *p* unlike trees *p* have more than one trunk *p* and they are also usually shorter than trees.
   (COMMAS AROUND INTERRUPTIONS)   (COMMA WITH COORDINATING CONJUNCTIONS)

Exercise 6.16 With a partner, find and correct the punctuation errors in the following sentences:

1. José and María my best friends have the same hobbies?

2. One of my best friends, now lives in Iran.

3. Nevertheless the politicians should try to pass the bill for it would give more money to education.

4. Most of the time these problems appear after the diamond is cut.

5. First of all whereas a good student likes to study and do all of the homework a bad student never worries about studying.

Exercise 6.17 Look through the assignments your instructor has returned to you from this class (or from any other class where your writing errors were identified). Find three punctuation errors in the assignments, and analyze them using the following chart.

Example

Error: ___When you finish here you can go home.___

p problem: ___I left out a comma.___

Rule: <u>If you start a sentence with a dependent clause, you must put a comma before</u>

<u>the independent clause.</u>

Correction: <u>When you finish here, you can go home.</u>

Fragments *(frag)*

Symbol	Meaning	Explanation
frag	Fragment	The sentence is incomplete.

Examples

Wrong: The man whom I saw yesterday.
frag
Correction: The man whom I saw yesterday **is his son.**

Wrong: When you come to class.
frag
Correction: When you come to class, **bring the pen.**

A fragment is an incomplete sentence. It lacks (needs) either a subject or a conjugated verb. In some fragments, a verb lacks an object. Subordinate clauses and prepositional phrases by themselves are also fragments. Look at the following fragments:

1. The spectacle of bullfighting, which is enjoyed in Spain, Mexico, and many South American countries.

2. When the picadors use the sharp steel-tipped pikes to weaken and anger the bull.

3. The banderilleros carrying sticks in each hand and sticking them in the bull's neck.

4. When bullfights take place in Seville.

Each of these sentences must have a subject and a conjugated verb. If the sentence contains an adjective clause, it must also contain an independent clause.

Possible Corrections

1. The spectacle of bullfighting ~~which~~ is enjoyed in Spain, Mexico, and many South American countries.

2. ~~When~~ The picadors use the sharp steel-tipped pikes to weaken and anger the bull.

3. The banderilleros carry~~ing~~ sticks in each hand and stick~~ing~~ them in the bull's neck.

4. ~~When~~ Some bullfights take place in Seville.

Exercise 6.18 Read the following paragraph aloud with a partner. Underline the fragments in the following paragraphs and then correct the paragraph.

Louis Armstrong, an American trumpet player. Was born on July 4, 1900, in New Orleans, the birthplace of American jazz. Louis went to school at the "Colored Waifs' Home for Boys." Where he learned to play several musical instruments. His favorite was the cornet, which he taught himself to play. He had a special talent for music. And became the leader of the school band. He later moved to Chicago.   Where he played in the King Oliver Band. Louis became the first internationally famous soloist in jazz. From 1925 to 1928. He made a series of records that are among the greatest in jazz history. Many people believe that Louis Armstrong was the greatest jazz musician of all time.

Exercise 6.19 Find three **fragments** in the assignments that have been returned to you, and analyze them as follows.

Example

Error: _____ Because I thought it was the right thing to do._____

frag **problem:** _____ I wrote a subordinate clause as a complete sentence._____

Rule: _____ When you have a dependent clause, you must also have an independent clause._____

Correction: _____ I did it because I thought it was the right thing to do._____

• Run-Ons

Symbol	Meaning	Explanation
ro	Run-on	The sentence is incorrectly connected to another sentence.

Examples

Wrong: It is raining we must take umbrellas.
                                        ro
Correction: It is raining, so we must take umbrellas.

Wrong: I like June she is nice she lives in L.A.

ro

Correction: I like June. She is nice. She lives in L.A.

● Comma Splices

Symbol	Meaning	Explanation
cs	Comma splice	Two independent clauses are incorrectly punctuated; they are separated only by a comma.

Examples

Wrong: It is raining, we must take umbrellas.

cs

Correction: It is raining, so we must take umbrellas.

Wrong: I like June, she is nice, she lives in L.A.

ro

Correction: I like June. She is nice. She lives in L.A.

When two or more independent clauses (complete sentences) are written as one sentence, without end punctuation, the sentence is called a "run-on" sentence. It is NOT correct. When the independent sentences are separated only by a comma with no connecting words, it is called a "comma splice." It is NOT correct. Run-on sentences and comma splices are common but serious errors in writing. Look at these sentences. They are WRONG.

Wrong: Sergio, for whom I voted, lost by three votes, people were surprised.

comma splice

Wrong: Sergio, for whom I voted, lost by three votes people were surprised.

run-on

You can correct a run-on sentence and comma splice with end punctuation or by connecting the two sentences with a connecting word.

Correction: Sergio, for whom I voted, lost by three votes, and people were surprised.

Correction: Sergio, for whom I voted, lost by three votes. People were surprised.

Exercise 6.20   Read this paragraph aloud with a partner. Use periods to correct the run-on sentences and comma splices.

Harriet Tubman was an American slave, she was born in 1820 on a plantation in Buckman, Maryland. When she was 13, she tried to free a slave from punishment, the supervisor fractured her skull. As a result of the injury to her head, she fell asleep suddenly several times a day for the rest of her life. Harriet hated slavery, when she was old enough, she escaped to Philadelphia, she traveled at night with the help of the underground railroad, a secret network of people who helped slaves reach the Northern states and Canada. Harriet worked as a maid, and she saved her money, then she made the first of 19 trips back to the south to lead slaves to freedom. With the help of the underground railroad, Harriet led more than 300 slaves to freedom, Harriet is still a symbol of hope and love for all people and especially blacks, her memory will live on forever.

Exercise 6.21   Find two **comma splice errors** and two **run-on errors** in assignments that have been returned to you, and analyze them using the following chart.

Example

Error: ___The girl was listening to the music, Jane was eating her lunch.___

cs problem: ___I used a comma to separate two complete sentences.___

Rule: ___You cannot separate two complete independent clauses with only a comma.___

Correction: ___The girl was listening to music. Jane was eating lunch.___

Example

Error: ___The girl was listening to the music Jane was eating her lunch.___

ro problem: ___I didn't use any punctuation to separate two complete sentences.___

Rule: ___You cannot write two complete independent clauses as one sentence.___

Correction: ___The girl was listening to music. Jane was eating lunch.___

Chapter One Supplement

TEN TOPIC SENTENCE "DON'T'S"

Don't #1: Don't write a fragment as a topic sentence.

Every topic sentence needs to have a complete subject and a conjugated verb. A fragment is an incomplete sentence because it lacks either the subject or the conjugated verb, or it begins with subordinating conjunctions, such as *after* or *because*.

Examples of "Don't"

1. My dog's loud bark. **(This sentence has no conjugated verb.)**

2. Living in a large city and raising children there. **(This sentence has no conjugated verb.)**

3. When it is raining and people's health is affected. **(This sentence has no independent clause.)**

Corrections

    1. My dog's bark can wake the dead.

    2. It can be difficult to raise a child in a large city.

    3. The excessive rain has affected people's health this winter.

Exercise S1.1   Write your own ORIGINAL corrections for these three examples:

1. _____

2. _____

3. _____

Don't #2: Don't announce the topic.

Don't write expressions like "This paragraph will discuss..." or "This is a description of..." in your topic sentence. The topic sentence needs a controlling idea that says something interesting and meaningful about the topic. It needs to catch the reader's attention. Topic sentences which only announce the topic sound dry and boring because they frequently omit the controlling idea.

Examples of "Don't"

1. I'm going to tell you about my dog's bark. **(Readers have no idea what the writer is going to say about the dog's bark because this sentence has no controlling idea.)**

2. This paragraph will discuss raising children in a city. **(Readers have an idea of what the paragraph will be about, but the topic sentence is boring and does not inspire the reader to continue.)**

3. Let me explain about DUI (Driving Under the Influence). **(This sentence has no controlling idea. The readers cannot see what the paragraph will say about drinking and driving—why you should not do it? what the legal definition of DUI is?)**

More Examples and Their Corrections

Bad: 1. This paragraph will discuss the death penalty.

Good: Anyone convicted of selling dangerous drugs to children should receive the death penalty.

Bad: 2. I am going to describe my grandmother in this paragraph.

Good: My grandmother was the most eccentric member of my family.

Bad: 3. Let me explain about registering early for classes.

Good: It is easy to register early for classes if you follow these simple steps.

Exercise S1.2 Write your own ORIGINAL corrections for these three examples:

1. I'm going to tell you about my writing teacher.

   _____

2. This paragraph will discuss the arguments against legalizing drugs in large cities.

   _____

3. Let me explain about this teacher's grading policies.

   _____

Don't #3: Don't state the topic sentence as a personal opinion.

When you write the words, "In my opinion" or "I believe," in your topic sentence, you weaken it. Academic paragraphs should be written objectively. When you sound as if you are offering your personal opinion, you invite your reader to disagree with you. Look at the following sentences. Which one do you feel is stronger? Which one do you feel you can disagree with?

> In my opinion, teachers of ESOL[1] should be required to learn a second language.
> Teachers of ESOL should be required to learn a second language.

It is true that the topic sentence usually reflects your opinion about a person, place, thing, or idea (the controlling idea does this), but you should write the topic sentence as an objective fact. That makes your paragraph more authoritative.

Examples of "Don't"

1. I believe that John Wayne was the best actor Hollywood ever produced. **(The topic sentence sounds weak.)**

2. In my opinion, writing poetry is fun. **(You invite your readers to give their own opinion of what is fun.)**

3. When you need to buy a car, I think you should go with a couple of friends. **(You do not sound like you are sure about what you are saying.)**

More Examples and Their Corrections

1. **I think that** the air pollution in Denver is slowly killing the citizens of that beautiful city.

1. ~~I think that~~ The air pollution in Denver is slowly killing the citizens of that beautiful city.

2. **In my opinion,** grades should be abolished in ESOL and foreign language classes.

2. ~~In my opinion,~~ Grades should be abolished in ESOL and foreign language classes.

3. **I believe that** all houses in Northern California should have brick fireplaces.

Exercise S1.3   Correct the third example (above) yourself:

_____

Don't #4: Don't include the paragraph's supporting ideas in the topic sentence.

The topic sentence should have only a topic and a controlling idea, written in a complete sentence. It should not contain supporting details that belong in the body of the paragraph. Notice that in the following sentences, the support is given in the first sentence. There is nothing left to write in the paragraph.

---

1 ESOL (English for Speakers of Other Languages), ESL (English as a Second Language), and EFL (English as a Foreign Language) all refer to teaching English to nonnative speakers of English.

Examples of "Don't"

1. Albert Einstein was considered a slow learner **because he didn't talk until he was three years old, he didn't learn to read until he was seven, and he never answered his teachers in class.**

2. Volunteering to help at the homeless shelter will be rewarding **because you will be helping people who really need help, you will meet a variety of interesting people from all walks of life, and you will be using your free time in a constructive and charitable way.**

3. If you want to format a computer disk on the Macintosh computer, **simply insert the disk, click on "erase" when you see the dialogue box, type a name for your disk if you want, and then click on "OK."**

Corrections

1. Amazingly, Albert Einstein was considered a slow learner.

2. Volunteering to help at the homeless shelter can be rewarding.

Exercise S1.4 Correct the third sentence above. Be careful not to write a FRAGMENT!!

3. _____

Don't #5: Don't forget to focus the topic.

In the following sentences, the topics are too general for one paragraph. The words used as focused topics could mean different things to different readers, so the author's message is not communicated effectively.

Examples of "Don't"

1. **People** have beautiful cars.
2. **Outdoor activities** can be dangerous.
3. **Education** is important.

Corrections

1. My sister has a beautiful car.
2. Some water sport activities can be dangerous unless you are careful.
3. Bilingual residents can benefit from earning a translation certificate.

Exercise S1.5 Look at the corrections for the following topic sentences. Then write a different correctly focused topic sentence for each one.

1. **Transportation** is important. **(What kind of transportation? Where?)**
   Correction: If you live in the country, it is essential to own a car or a truck.

   Your correction: _____

2. Crime is a problem for people. **(What kind of crime? Murder? Shoplifting?)**
   Correction: Shoplifting has caused the prices of merchandise at Midway Mall to increase for three reasons.

   Your correction: _____

3. Animals are great pets. **(What kind of animal? Dogs? Lizards?)**
   Correction: A Vietnamese potbelly pig can be a great house pet.

   Your correction: _____

Don't #6: Don't write more than one focused topic in the topic sentence.

A paragraph of comparison/contrast may have two different topics. In most other paragraphs, you may only have ONE topic.

Examples of "Don't"

1. New York and Los Angeles are beautiful cities at night. **(This topic sentence would require two paragraphs.)**

2. Traveling to Mexico or France can be exciting. **(This topic sentence would also require two paragraphs.)**

3. Registering early for classes and applying for financial aid are complicated procedures. **(Each of these topics would require a separate paragraph.)**

Corrections

1. New York is a beautiful city at night.

Exercise S1.6 Correct the second and third examples above.

2. _____

3. _____

Don't #7: Don't omit the topic.

When students write titles for paragraphs, they sometimes forget that the focused topic must also appear in the topic sentence. A good way to avoid this problem is to write the paragraph first, and then, if your teacher insists on a title for the paragraph, use your focused topic from the topic sentence for your title.

Examples of "Don't"

1. **She** is the best actress in my country. **(Who is the writer talking about?)**

2. **This** is a waste of time and of money. **(What is the writer talking about?)**

3. **It** can cause serious problems for this college. **(What is the problem?)**

Correction

1. Isabel Torres is the best actress in my country.

Exercise S1.7 Correct the three examples by adding a logical topic to each sentence:

1. _____

2. _____

3. _____

Don't #8: Don't omit the controlling idea.

If you omit the controlling idea, your topic sentence may sound like a simple fact that does not need supporting sentences for explanation. Your topic sentence will not tell the reader what to expect in your paragraph.

Examples of "Don't"

1. The sun is the center of our solar system.

2. Birds have wings and beaks.

3. The weather in Canada is cold in the winter.

Correction

1. There are three ways to protect yourself from the sun's ultraviolet rays when you go to the beach.

Exercise S1.8 Correct the three examples by adding a logical controlling idea to each sentence:

1. _____

2. _____

3. _____

Don't #9: Don't write more than one controlling idea.

Each paragraph should develop only one controlling idea, so be sure that you do not write more than one controlling idea in your topic sentence. In each of the following topic sentences, the controlling ideas would require more than one paragraph.

Examples of "Don't"

1. An ant is an industrious worker and a strange-looking insect. **(One paragraph could explain "industrious worker," and a separate paragraph could explain "strange-looking," but these adjectives are not synonyms, so they cannot BOTH be the controlling idea for a single paragraph.)**

2. Riding a motorcycle can be lots of fun, and it can be dangerous and expensive. **(This topic sentence contains three different controlling ideas. They are not synonyms. The sentence would require three paragraphs.)**

3. Preparing adequately for an exam can be easy, and it is important for three reasons. **(At first this topic sentence introduces a process, but then it introduces the idea of "reasons." This topic sentence would require two separate paragraphs.)**

Exercise S1.9 Correct the three examples by eliminating one of the controlling ideas from each sentence:

1. _____

2. _____

3. _____

Don't #10: Don't use vague words as controlling ideas.

It is important to select the very best and most descriptive adjective you can find for your controlling idea. Avoid controlling ideas that do not give the reader a clear picture of what you are going to say about the focused topic. Words such as "good," "bad," "nice," and "interesting" are not very descriptive. Notice the difference in the images that you see in the following topic sentences.

Examples of "Don't"

1. Fernando is a nice person. **(This controlling idea "nice" does not describe "Fernando" adequately. There are many more descriptive adjectives that could be used as the controlling idea to give the reader a better idea of Fernando's personality.)**

2. Lorraine is an interesting girl. **(The controlling idea "interesting" is too general. You can use it in your paragraph, but not as the controlling idea in the topic sentence.)**

3. Professor Jones is a bad teacher. **(There are many more descriptive controlling ideas than "bad.")**

Corrections

Fernando is a **nice person.**
{
Fernando has *romantic eyes.*
Fernando has a *fantastic physique.*
Fernando is a *gentle person.*

Lorraine is an **interesting girl.**
{
Lorraine is *the most intelligent* student in our class.
Lorraine is *the most eccentric* person I know.
Lorraine is *crazy.*

Professor Jones is a **bad teacher.**
{
Professor Jones's *explanations in class are unclear.*
Professor Jones *is hard to understand.*
Professor Jones is *unsympathetic to students who are nonnative speakers of English.*

Exercise S1.10 Write your own ORIGINAL corrections for these three examples:

1. _____

2. _____

3. _____

Exercise S1.11 Each of these topic sentences has an error, which is given in parentheses. Rewrite the topic sentences. Make sure each sentence is complete and that it has only one topic. Check to see that the topic is adequately focused, that each sentence has only one controlling idea, and that the controlling idea is interesting and limited enough to develop with three supporting ideas. Also make sure that each sentence is grammatically correct.

1. (unfocused topic) People should learn a second language.

   _____

2. (fragment) How to wash a dog in three easy steps.

   _____

3. (no topic) That is the worst restaurant in Miami.

   _____

4. (vague controlling idea) Sharon is nice.

   _____

5. (boring topic) I need some new shoes.

   _____

6. (two controlling ideas) This writing class is challenging and it is fun.

   _____

7. (no controlling idea) It is raining outside.

   _____

EDITING SYMBOLS

This section is a reference list for the editing symbols that are presented at the end of each chapter in the text. Your teacher may use some of these symbols on your writing assignments to indicate the types of errors you have made. You can use this list to see what those symbols mean. You can find more exercises for each type of error in the Editing Symbols exercises at the end of each chapter.

The first part of the section gives definitions of each symbol and examples of each kind of error. The second part is a checklist you can use to keep track of your own errors on writing assignments. As your instructor returns your corrected writing assignments, put check marks beside the symbols that represent the types of errors you have made. If you consistently make certain errors, ask your instructor for additional help in those areas.

Editing Symbols—Definitions

• Problems with Paragraph Form

Symbol	Meaning	Explanation
¶	New paragraph	Start a new paragraph (INDENT).
¶̷ OR **no** ¶	No new paragraph	Do NOT start a new paragraph here.

Example

¶ >
> > > > > > >. >.
> >
> >. >
> > > > > > > > > > > > > > >. >
> > > > > > >. >
> > > >. >. > >
> >.

• Problems with Topic Sentence (*ts*)

Symbol	Meaning	Explanation
foc	Focus	The topic is not focused. It is too general for one paragraph.

Example: **People** need to learn the language of that country quickly.

Symbol	Meaning	Explanation
ci	Controlling idea	The controlling idea is weak, missing, or not developed in the paragraph.

Example: Jorge Luis Borges is a **nice** author.

Symbol	Meaning	Explanation
off topic	Off topic	The topic of the topic sentence is not the same as the topic of the paragraph.

Example: ...**My father** has a wonderful smile. **My mother** has a nice personality....

Problems with Sentence Connecting

Symbol	Meaning	Explanation
p	Punctuation	The sentence has an error in punctuation.

Example: If it rains I will get wet.

Symbol	Meaning	Explanation
frag	Fragment	The sentence is incomplete.

Example: When you come to class.

Symbol	Meaning	Explanation
ro	Run-on	The sentence is incorrectly connected to another sentence.

Example: It is raining we must take umbrellas.

Symbol	Meaning	Explanation
cs	Comma splice	Two independent clauses are incorrectly punctuated: they are separated only by a comma.

Example: It is raining, we must take umbrellas.

Problems with Sentences (Grammar and Syntax)

Symbol	Meaning	Explanation
ps	Parallel structure	The sentence does not have parallel structure.

Example: I like to **swim, fishing,** and **jogging.**

Symbol	Meaning	Explanation
wo	Word order	The word order is wrong.

Example: Give **to me the ball blue.**

Symbol	Meaning	Explanation
ss	Sentence structure	The sentence structure contains an error.

Example: She is absent **because of she is sick.**

Symbol	Meaning	Explanation
(sv) agr	Subject-verb agreement	The subject and verb do not agree.

Example: **He go** early to class on Mondays.

Symbol	Meaning	Explanation
(pron) agr	Pronoun agreement	The pronoun does not agree with the subject.

Example: **Everyone** likes to drive **their** car.

Symbol	Meaning	Explanation
(#) agr	Number agreement	The word is plural and should be singular or vice versa.

Example: **These book** are mine.

Symbol	Meaning	Explanation
vt	Verb tense	The verb tense is wrong.

Example: When you **will** arrive, we can leave.

Symbol	Meaning	Explanation
shift	Shift	The pronoun, tense, or number is not consistent.

Example: **People** need love because **you** can't grow up without it.

Symbol	Meaning	Explanation
^	Omission	A word has been omitted here.

Example: When ^ you going to return to Peru?

Problems with Words

Symbol	Meaning	Explanation
sp	Spelling	The word is not spelled correctly.

Example: Is this **there** pen or **hour** pen?

Symbol	Meaning	Explanation
ww	Wrong word	The word is not used logically.

Example: I want to **take** some water. I **have** thirst.

Symbol	Meaning	Explanation
wf	Word form	The word is written in the wrong form (adverb, adjective, noun).

Example: Hank sings **good.**

Symbol	Meaning	Explanation
?? (logic)	Unclear	This part (word, sentence, section) is unclear.

Example: **We have fished the tree too green.**

SELF-EDITING CHECKLIST

ASSIGNMENTS:	1	2	3	4	5	6
Paragraph form						
¶						
¶ OR **no ¶**						
Topic sentence						
foc						
ci						
off topic						
Sentence connecting						
p						
frag						
ro						
cs						
Grammar and syntax						
ps						
wo						
ss						
agr						
vt						
shift						
^						
Word errors						
sp						
ww						
wf						
Unclear logic						
logic (??)						

Chapter Two Supplement

FOUR STEPS TO ADJECTIVE CLAUSES

To create an adjective clause, you must have at least two sentences which share a common noun. Then follow four steps.

Step #1

Determine which element in the first sentence is repeated in the second sentence. (In the first sentence, this word is called the **antecedent.**)

Examples

I see **a man.**　　**The man** is working on his car.
ANTECEDENT

I see **a man.**　　I spoke to **that man** yesterday.
ANTECEDENT

Step #2

Replace the repeated word in the second sentence with one of these words (relative pronouns):

who	for a person (subject of the second sentence)
whom	for a person (object of the second sentence **with its preposition)**
which	for a thing
whose	for a possessive word (Put the object that is possessed directly after "whose.")
where	for a place (The place must be used in the sentence as a location and not as an object.)
when	for time
that	for a person or a thing

Examples

I see a man.   SUBJECT
                 The man is working on his car.
                 WHO

I see a man.   OBJECT
                 I spoke to **that man** yesterday.
                 TO WHOM

Step #3

After substituting (replacing) the relative pronoun for the repeated element in the second sentence, put that relative pronoun at the beginning of its sentence (the second sentence) and eliminate the repeated element.

I see a man.   ~~The man~~ is working on his car.
                 WHO

I see the man.   I spoke ~~to that man~~ yesterday.
                 TO WHOM
I see the man.   **TO WHOM** I spoke yesterday.

Step #4

Place the second sentence (now called the **relative clause** or **adjective clause**) directly **after** the **antecedent** in the first sentence. Be sure to finish writing the last part of the first sentence after you insert the relative clause in the sentence!!!

Examples

I see a man. He is working on his car.
I see a man **who** is working on his car.

I see a man. I spoke to that man yesterday.
I see the man **to whom** I spoke yesterday.

The man was fixing my father's car. I spoke to that man yesterday.
The man **to whom** I spoke yesterday *was fixing my father's car.*

Exercise S2.1

Underline the adjective clause in each sentence.

1. John Wayne, who has now passed away, performed in western movies in the United States.

2. John Wayne was an actor whom almost everybody admired.

3. The house that was recently built on the next block has a white picket fence.

4. There is the young man who was elected president of our German Club.

PRACTICE WITH ADJECTIVE CLAUSES

Who

If the word that you are replacing with the relative pronoun is a person, and it is the subject of its sentence, use *who* or *that*.

Examples

He is the man.   **The man** has a large briefcase.
                  SUBJECT

He is the man **who** has a large briefcase.
              SUBJECT PRONOUN

He is the man **that** has a large briefcase.
              SUBJECT PRONOUN

Who can be singular or plural. If the noun or pronoun before *who* is singular, then *who* is singular; if the noun or pronoun before *who* is plural, then *who* is plural.

Examples

Are they the **men**? **They work** downtown.
                      PLURAL
Are they the **men who work** downtown?
Are they the **men that work** downtown?

He is the man. **He works** downtown.
               SINGULAR
He is the **man who works** downtown.
He is the **man that works** downtown.

Exercise S2.2   Combine each pair of sentences into one sentence using *who*.

1. Do you see the woman? / She was buying groceries at Safeway.

   _____

2. We saw three women. / They were robbing a bank.

   _____

3. Is that child nearsighted? / She is wearing thick glasses.

   _____

4. The teacher was fired. / He never came to class on time.

   _____

5. Do the students receive bad grades? / They don't do their homework.

   _____

Whom

If the word that you are replacing with the relative pronoun is a person, and it is the object in its sentence, use *whom, that,* or no pronoun (the object pronoun can be omitted from an adjective clause).

Examples

They are the men. We spoke **to them** yesterday.
                                OBJECT
They are the men **to whom** we spoke yesterday.
They are the men ___ we spoke to yesterday.

Was that person absent today? We saw **that person** here yesterday.
                                        OBJECT
Was that person **whom** we saw here yesterday absent today?
Was that person ___ we saw here yesterday absent today?

Exercise S2.3   Combine each pair of sentences into a single sentence using *whom*.

1. The people live in Minnesota. / Karen is visiting them next month.

   _____

2. Do you remember the man? / We met him on the trip to Canada.

   _____

3. I don't know any of the students. / The teacher is talking about them.

_____

4. Are they the people? / My father knows them.

_____

5. Those people are odd but friendly. / I live near them.

_____

Whose

   If the word that you are replacing with the relative pronoun is a possessive word such as *his, her, its, John's,* or *of the car,* use *whose.* When you use *whose,* be sure that the object that is possessed follows *whose* in the adjective clause. *Whose* is used for people or things.

Examples

   This is the computer. I removed **its** hard disk yesterday.
   This is the computer **whose**[1] hard disk I removed yesterday.

   People are unhappy. **Their taxes** increased last year.
   People **whose taxes** increased last year are unhappy.

Exercise S2.4   Combine each pair of sentences into a single sentence using *whose.*

1. Teachers are well respected. / Their grading procedures are fair and flexible.

_____

2. Dogs are hard to groom. / Their fur is very long and silky.

_____

3. A classmate was absent from class. / We saw her car parked on the freeway this morning.

_____

4. A house is not safe. / The house's front door has no lock.

_____

5. You cannot ride a bicycle. / Its tires are flat.

_____

_____

1 Note that *whose* replaces a possessive word that refers to a person OR A THING.

Which

If the word that you are replacing with the relative pronoun is a thing (subject or object), use *which* or *that*. When you replace an object, the pronoun can be omitted, but when you replace a subject, the pronoun may not be omitted.

Examples

Elections are important in a democracy. **Elections** are correctly conducted.
Elections **which** are correctly conducted are important in a democracy.
Elections **that** are correctly conducted are important in a democracy.

Wrong: Elections are correctly conducted are important in a democracy.

The elections were televised on CBS. We held **elections** in Los Angeles.
The elections **which** we held in Los Angeles were televised on CBS.
The elections **that** we held in Los Angeles were televised on CBS.
The elections ___ we held in Los Angeles were televised on CBS.

Exercise S2.5   Combine each pair of sentences into a single sentence using *which* or *that*.

1. The movie was full of adventure and excitement. We saw it last Friday.

   _____

2. Don't you speak a language? That language has fewer vowel sounds than English.

   _____

3. The sandwich was delicious. I had it for lunch.

   _____

4. Did you lose the watch? You borrowed it from me yesterday.

   _____

5. The exam was very difficult. We took it last week.

   _____

Exercise S2.6   Change *that* to *who, whom,* or *which*. Also, omit *that* if possible.

1. The pizza that we cooked for dinner was not as good as the pizza that we ate last week.

   _____

2. I like movies that I can watch with friends that visit us on the weekends.

_____

3. I don't know anyone that I can practice Russian with.

_____

4. People that do not respect the basic rights of others should be removed from society.

_____

5. People that can't read or write have few job opportunities in this country.

_____

Exercise S2.7 Complete these sentences with an appropriate and logical adjective clause to describe the noun (the last word in each sentence below). Use *who, whom,* or *which* to create an adjective clause for each sentence.

Example

Teenagers like music...

Teenagers like music _which is loud and has a good beat._____

1. Do you want a teacher...

_____

2. Everyone wants a boss...

_____

3. Do you want to buy a house...

_____

4. I would love to have a friend...

_____

5. Don't teachers like students...

_____

Exercise S2.8   Add an adjective clause to each sentence.

Example

The thief was captured.

He robbed the bank.

> The thief who robbed the bank was captured.
>
> **or**
>
> The thief that robbed the bank was captured.

The thief was captured.

1. His car had a flat tire.

   _____

2. We hear about him on the news.

   _____

3. I told you about the thief.

   _____

4. Bob knew the thief personally.

   _____

5. We saw his picture on television.

   _____

Exercise S2.9   Combine the following sentences by making the **second** sentence into an adjective clause.

1. We enjoy meeting new students. These students come from all over the world.

   _____

2. Didn't we complete a lesson last week? That lesson was on sentence connectors.

   _____

3. Do most South Americans speak Spanish? That Spanish is different from that spoken in Spain.

   _____

4. Are there many students? Those students have good grades in this class.

_____

5. Is this the child? Her dog ran away.

_____

ABOUT PUNCTUATION OF ADJECTIVE CLAUSES

If the antecedent (the word that is being modified by an adjective clause) is a proper noun or a noun that does not require the adjective clause for identification purposes, then the adjective clause is set off by commas; there is a comma in front of the relative pronoun and another comma after the adjective clause.

Mary, who is my best friend, lives near McKinleyville.

In this sentence, *Mary* is a proper noun. The information in the adjective clause is not used to identify "which Mary" the sentence is talking about. In sentences like this, the commas are used because the information is not essential to identify the subject of the main clause, so the reader pauses when beginning and ending the adjective clause. The commas represent those pauses in speech.

The girl who is my best friend lives near McKinleyville.

In this sentence, the information in the adjective clause is used to tell the reader "which girl" the sentence is talking about. The adjective clause is used to identify the subject in the main clause. Here no comma is needed. There is no pause in the reader's voice when reading the sentence, and the adjective clause becomes part of the subject of the sentence. Read both of the preceding examples aloud and notice that the pauses in the first sentence do not occur in the second.

Add commas where necessary in the following sentences:

1. Alfonso who is on the swim team for this college is from Venezuela.

2. One person who is on the swim team for this college is from Venezuela.

3. A teacher whom everyone in the school respects is Professor Jones.

4. Our speech teacher whom everyone in the class respects has written several books and articles.

5. Marco whose brother is a professional boxer in Puerto Rico will be leaving town for two weeks.

Exercise S2.10   Add an adjective clause with correct punctuation where you see the blanks. You will need to rewrite the sentences because they may be long.

Example

Juan _____ works in a company _____ .

    Juan, _who lives in Texas with my family,_ works in a company _which produces_ _computer chips for Sony_ .

1. María _____ has a beautiful smile _____ .

_____

2. Susan's parents _____ do not like to visit the beaches _____ .

_____

3. Steven _____ always helps his classmates _____ with their writing assignments.

_____

4. A woman _____ is popular with men _____ .

_____

5. A student _____ reads books _____ .

_____

Exercise S2.11   Look at one of the paragraphs you did for the exercises in this or the previous chapter. Add adjective clauses to the secondary support. Make sure the adjective clauses help develop the controlling idea of the paragraph, and check the punctuation of each one. Give both the old and the new paragraphs to your teacher.

Chapter Three Supplement

SENTENCE PATTERNS FOR COMPARISON PARAGRAPHS

Five Sentence Patterns for Topic Sentences

If you **do not** need to focus your topic, you can use one of the first three patterns. These three patterns do not name specific aspects, such as "geographic location" or "physical characteristics," that will be compared. They use the words *ways* or *similarities* instead.

Study each pattern, and then do the writing exercise that follows with a partner.

● **Pattern #1**

X and Y (be) similar in (#) [adjective] ways.

X and Y (be) alike in (#) [adjective] ways.

Examples

Rhinos and hippos are similar in three strange ways.
    X   AND   Y   (BE) SIMILAR IN   (#) [ADJECTIVE] WAYS.

Rhinos and hippos are alike in three strange ways.
    X   AND   Y   (BE) ALIKE IN   (#) [ADJECTIVE] WAYS.

The subject in this pattern is always compound, so the verb is always plural.

Exercise S3.1 Write topic sentences using sentence pattern #1 and the topics given.

Example

love and hate

___Although you may not believe it, the two strongest human emotions, love and hate,___

___are similar in many ways.___

1. donkeys / horses

_____

2. carne mechada, a typical dish in Juan's country / ropa vieja, a typical dish in Francisco's country

_____

3. the gymnasium / the library

_____

● Pattern #2

X **(be)** *similar to Y in* **(#)** **[adjective]** *ways.*

X **(be)** *like Y in* **(#)** **[adjective]** *ways.*

Examples

Dogs are similar to wolves in five important ways.
  X   (BE) SIMILAR TO   Y   IN (#) [ADJECTIVE]   WAYS.

Soup is like stew in three delicious ways.
  X   (BE) LIKE   Y   IN   (#)   [ADJECTIVE]   WAYS.

This topic sentence pattern is similar to pattern #1. The difference is that instead of writing "X and Y are similar," you write "X is similar to Y." This means that the verb can be singular or plural depending on "X." You can use *similar to* or *like* in the pattern. Remember that *like* does not take *to* in this sentence pattern.

      Wrong: Dog are similar to wolf in five important ways.
      Correct: Dogs are similar to wolves in five important ways.

      Wrong: Dogs are like ~~to~~ wolves in five important ways.
      Correct: Dogs are like wolves in five important ways.

Exercise S3.2 Write topic sentences using sentence pattern #2 and the topics given.

Examples

a hurricane / a tornado

    a. (similar to)   A hurricane is similar to a tornado in three dangerous ways.

    b. (like) A hurricane is like a tornado in three important ways.

1. a river / a stream

    a. (similar to) _____

    b. (like) _____

2. the IBM computer / the Macintosh computer

    a. (similar to) _____

    b. (like) _____

● Pattern #3

There are (#) [adjective] similarities between X and Y.

Example

There are some amazing similarities between dolphins and humans.
THERE ARE   (#)   [ADJ.]   SIMILARITIES BETWEEN   X   AND   Y.

This topic sentence pattern is an easy one to use. It uses *there are* and the word *similarities,* but you should add a number word *(some, several, a few, three)* and/or an adjective to make the topic sentence clear.

Exercise S3.3 Write topic sentences using sentence pattern #3 and the topics given.

Example

Abraham Lincoln and John F. Kennedy

    There are many strange similarities between the deaths of Abraham Lincoln

    and John F. Kennedy.

1. the system of transportation in my hometown / the system of transportation in this city

   _____

2. snow / hail

   _____

3. the moon / the earth

   _____

If you need to focus your topic, you can use either of the two patterns below. Notice how each pattern names a specific noun (not *way* or *similarity*) that will be compared.

● Pattern #4

X and Y **[verb]** ~~(not be)~~ **(#)** *similar* **[noun(s)].**

X and Y **[verb]** ~~(not be)~~ *a similar* **[noun] (singular/non-count).**

Do not use "be" in these patterns.

Examples

Smoking and breathing secondhand smoke can cause similar health problems.
    X   AND   Y   [VERB]   SIMILAR   [NOUN].

In the body of this paragraph, the writer will focus exclusively on the health problems that smoking and breathing smoke can cause.

Carlos and Marcos have a similar cultural heritage.
    X   AND   Y   [VERB] A SIMILAR   [NOUN].

What will this paragraph focus on? Will it describe Carlos's and Marcos's personalities?

John and Steven share three dreadful qualities.
    X   AND   Y   SHARE   [#]   [ADJECTIVE] [NOUN].

What will this paragraph focus on? Why will this paragraph be interesting to read?

These sentence patterns do not use "be" or "ways." They use nouns which are aspects of the topic that the writer will explain in the paragraph. In the examples above, "X and Y's" *health problems, cultural heritage,* and *dreadful qualities* will be compared in the body of the paragraphs.

Exercise S3.4 Write topic sentences using sentence pattern #4 and the topics given. Do not use the verb *be* in these sentences.

Example

> my aunt and my uncle
>
> My aunt and my uncle share the same basic religious beliefs.

1. drinking alcohol / taking drugs

   _____

2. José / Raul

   _____

3. driving a car / driving a small truck

   _____

● Pattern #5

X [be] *similar to Y with respect to* [noun phrase].

Example

Henry is similar to Tom with respect to personality.

X   [BE]   SIMILAR TO   Y   WITH RESPECT TO   [NOUN PHRASE].

In the body of this paragraph, the writer will focus on three aspects of the boys' personalities that are similar.

There are two important parts to this sentence pattern. The first uses *similar to* and the names of both "X" and "Y." The second part of the sentence gives the point of comparison. After the words *with respect to* you can write a noun or a noun phrase, not a complete sentence.

> **Wrong:** Henry is similar to Tom with respect to they are the same age.
> **Correct:** Henry is similar to Tom with respect to age.

Exercise S3.5 Write topic sentences using sentence pattern #5 and the topics given.

1. Mary / Sally

   _____

2. French restaurants / Italian restaurants

   _____

3. newspapers / magazines

Seven Sentence Patterns for the Body of the Paragraph

You can use the following sentence patterns in the body of your paragraph to introduce each support (if you include a transitional word or expression) or to add secondary support to your main points.

● Pattern #1

X **[verb]** *the same* **[noun (phrase)]** *as* **[noun (phrase)]** **[auxiliary].**

Examples

Jane wears almost the same hairstyle as Mary (as Mary does).
   X   [VERB]   THE SAME   [NOUN]   AS [NOUN].

That class has taken the same number of exams as we (as we have).
     X   [VERB]   THE SAME   [NOUN]   AS [NOUN].

I speak the same language as my father (as my father speaks/as my father does).
X [VERB] THE SAME   [NOUN]   AS   [NOUN].

This sentence pattern sometimes confuses students because it uses a NOUN and not an adjective in the comparison. This is because the main verb is not *be*. Note above that the second part of the sentence has several options. You can include the auxiliary verb to complete the comparison, or simply use "Y."

    Wrong: Jane has almost the same pretty as Mary.
    Correct: Jane has almost the same type of personality as Mary.

    Wrong: This test is almost the same difficult as that test.
    Correct: This test has almost the same level of difficulty as that one.

Exercise S3.6 Write sentences with the words given using sentence pattern #1.

Example

(Frank and John) type of student

Frank is the same type of student as John (is).

1. (my sister and I) height

    _____

2. (this class and that class) the same textbook

    _____

3. (The United States and Canada) types of natural resources

    _____

Complete the following sentences logically (use a noun).

4. My cousin likes to eat _____ as my uncle.

5. This country has _____ as my own country.

6. Dogs have _____ as cats do.

Pattern #2

X [be] *similar to Y in that* [clause].

X [be] *like Y in that* [clause].

Examples

Los Angeles is similar to New York in that both cities have wonderful theaters.
X (BE) SIMILAR TO Y IN THAT   [CLAUSE].

Los Angeles is like New York in that both cities have wonderful theaters.
X (BE) LIKE Y IN THAT   [CLAUSE].

There are two important parts to this sentence pattern. The first uses *similar to* or *like* and names both "X" and "Y." The second part of the sentence gives the point of comparison. After the words *in that* you must write a complete clause that again names "X" or both "X" and "Y."

Wrong: Los Angeles is similar to New York *in that very large and beautiful.*
Wrong: Los Angeles is similar to New York *in it is very large and beautiful.*
Wrong: Los Angeles is similar to New York *in they are both very large and beautiful.*

Correct: Los Angeles is similar to New York ***in that it is*** *very large and beautiful.*
Correct: Los Angeles is similar to New York ***in that they are*** *both very large and beautiful.*

Exercise S3.7 Write sentences with the words given using sentence pattern #2.

Example

(Frank and John) serious students

Frank is similar to John in that both are serious students.

1. (Sharon and Luanne) tall

2. (this class and that class) the same textbook

3. (Mexico and Canada) North America

● Pattern #3

Like X, (sentence about Y).

Examples

Like Francia, Adriana lives in Kendall with her family.

LIKE   X   ,   (COMPLETE SENTENCE ABOUT "Y").

In this pattern, the information in the second part of the sentence must be identical for both "X" and "Y." Also, you do not need to repeat the first noun ("X") in the second part of the sentence.

> **Wrong:** Like Francia, Adriana lives in almost the same kind of house as Francia.
> **Wrong:** Like Francia, Adriana and Francia live in a small townhouse.
>
> **Correct:** Like Francia, Adriana lives in a small townhouse.

Exercise S3.8 Write sentences with the words given using sentence pattern #3.

Example

(the previous exercise, this exercise) comparisons

Like the previous exercise, this exercise teaches comparisons.

1. (Alaska, Canada) cold in winter

   _____

2. (the Rockies, the Appalachians) high

   _____

3. (a verb, a noun) a part of speech

   _____

● Pattern #4

(sentence about _X_), _and so_ (auxiliary) _Y_ [as subject].
(sentence about _X_), _and_ _Y_ [as subject] (auxiliary) _too_.
(sentence about _X_), _but_ _Y_ [as subject] (auxiliary).

When two affirmative sentences give the same information about two different subjects, you can connect the sentences with _so_ or _too_. The action in both sentences must be identical. If one sentence is affirmative and the other negative, you should use a word like _but_ or _however_ to show the contrast. _So_ goes at the beginning of the attached sentence; _too_ goes at the end.

Examples

John lives here, and so   does   Henry.
(SENTENCE)   AND SO (AUXILIARY) Y [SUBJECT].

John lives here,   and Henry   does   too.
(SENTENCE ABOUT X),   AND Y [SUBJECT] (AUXILIARY) TOO.

John lives here, but   I   don't.
(SENTENCE ABOUT X), BUT   Y [SUBJECT]   (AFFIRMATIVE AUXILIARY).

John doesn't live here, but   I   do.
(SENTENCE ABOUT X),   BUT   Y [SUBJECT] (AFFIRMATIVE AUXILIARY).

More Examples

John is blond. Mark is blond.
    John is blond, and **so** is Mark.
    John is blond, and Mark is **too**.
    John is blond, **but** Mark's hair is black.

Mary has a Chevrolet. Shirley has a Chevrolet.
    Mary has a Chevrolet, and **so** does Shirley.
    Mary has a Chevrolet, and Shirley does **too**.
    Mary has a Chevrolet, **but** Shirley has a Ford.

Exercise S3.9

Part 1 Answer these questions about yourself in complete sentences.

1. What do you like to eat when you go out for dinner?

   _____

2. Where does your best friend like to go on his/her vacations?

   _____

3. Does your favorite classmate come to school on Mondays?

   _____

4. Do your parents visit you from time to time?

   _____

5. What kind of music do you like to listen to?

   _____

6. Where are you from?

   _____

Part 2 Now sit with a classmate and read him/her each of your sentences. After you read a sentence ask, "What about you?" Your classmate must answer using *so, too,* or *but.*

Example

> **You:** "I like to eat seafood when I go out to dinner. What about you?"
>
> **Your classmate:** "So do I."
>
> **OR** "I do too."
>
> **OR** "I don't."

Part 3 Write complete sentences about yourself and your partner using the information you have learned. Use *so, too,* or *but* in each sentence.

Example

I like to eat seafood when I go out to dinner, but my classmate doesn't.
_____

1. _____

2. _____

3. _____

4. _____

5. _____

6. _____

● Pattern #5

When two negative sentences give the same information about two different subjects, connect the sentences with *neither* or *either*. The sentences must both be negative, and the action in the sentences must be identical. *Neither* goes at the beginning of the attached sentence; *either* goes at the end. Notice that the attached sentence with *neither* takes an affirmative auxiliary, while the attached sentence with *either* takes a negative auxiliary. If a negative sentence is connected to an affirmative, use *but*.

(sentence about *X*), *and neither* (affirmative auxiliary) *Y* [as subject].

(negative sentence about *X*), *and Y* [as subject] (negative auxiliary) *either*.

(affirmative sentence about *X*), *but Y* [as subject] (affirmative auxiliary).

Examples

John doesn't live here, and neither   does   Henry.
(SENTENCE ABOUT X),   AND NEITHER (AFFIRMATIVE AUXILIARY) Y [SUBJECT].

John doesn't live here,   and Henry   doesn't   either.
(NEGATIVE SENTENCE ABOUT X), AND Y [SUBJECT] (NEGATIVE AUXILIARY)   EITHER.

John doesn't live here,   but   Henry   does.
(AFFIRMATIVE SENTENCE ABOUT X),   BUT   Y [AS SUBJECT]   (AFFIRMATIVE AUXILIARY).

More Examples

Larry hasn't finished this lesson. Bert hasn't finished this lesson.

    Larry hasn't finished this lesson, and **neither** has Bert.

    Larry hasn't finished this lesson, and Bert hasn't **either.**

    Larry hasn't finished this lesson, **but** Bert has.

Marie isn't ready to leave yet.   Carol isn't ready to leave yet.

   Marie isn't ready to leave yet, and **neither** is Carol.

   Marie isn't ready to leave yet, and Carol isn't **either.**

   Marie isn't ready to leave yet, **but** Carol is.

Exercise S3.10   Tell about yourself by adding an attached statement, using *but, either,* or *neither.*

Examples

My teacher never leaves class early, <u>and I don't either.</u>

My teacher never leaves class early, <u>and neither do I.</u>

My teacher never leaves class early, <u>but I do.</u>

1. Tom never hands in his homework on time, _____.

2. Lisa never raises her hand in class, _____.

3. Henry doesn't come late to class, _____.

4. You are not a bad singer, _____.

5. They don't chew gum in this class, _____.

Exercise S3.11   Write complete sentences using the following elements. The second part of the sentence will be an attached statement with *so, too, neither, either,* or *but.* Notice that some of the sentences will be negative.

1. electricity / be / important / daily life————indoor plumbing (too)

   _____

2. house / burn down————barn (but)

   _____

3. that restaurant / serve / delicious steak————this restaurant (so)

   _____

4. Lee / catch / many salmon————Max (neither)

   _____

5. Dennis / arrive / on time————Roxanne (either)

_____

● Pattern #6

both, both...and

You can use *both* or *both...and* in affirmative sentences to indicate a similarity. The position of *both* is flexible, and it can modify different parts of your sentence. The verb that follows *both* is plural.

Examples

Both you and I love living here in South Florida.

They are both guilty. Both of them are guilty. Both are guilty.

You and I are both here. **Both of us** are here. **Both you and I** are here.

We like to watch **both television and movies.** **(modifies "television and movies")**

Both of us like to watch television and movies. **(modifies "us")**

We both like to watch television and movies. **(modifies "we")**

You can put **both sugar and cream** in the coffee. **(modifies "sugar and cream")**

● Pattern #7

neither...nor

You can use *neither...nor* to make a negative comparison. The position of *neither* depends on which elements of the sentence you want to compare. The verb that follows *nor* agrees in number (is plural or singular) with the subject that is after *nor*. However, when you want to use both a plural and a singular noun with the *neither...nor* sentence pattern, you should put the plural noun after *nor*.

Examples

My mother is not here. My sister is not here.

Neither my mother nor *my sister* **is** here.
SINGULAR

Neither my mother nor *my sisters* **are** here.
PLURAL

Neither ~~my sisters nor my mother~~ are here. **(Always put the plural noun last.)**

Exercise S3.12 Combine the following sentences with *both, both...and,* or *neither...nor.*

1. The captain was here yesterday. The lieutenant was here yesterday.

   _____

2. They couldn't talk about it. We couldn't talk about it.

   _____

3. Space is an unexplored frontier. The ocean bottom is an unexplored frontier.

   _____

4. The radio did not report the crime. The television didn't report the crime.

   _____

5. I turned off the heater. I turned off the lights.

   _____

6. We took our guests to the zoo. We took our guests to the Seaquarium.

   _____

7. We don't go to the beach during the week. We don't go to the zoo during the week.

   _____

8. We went to the museum. We went to the theater.

   _____

9. The dog was not vaccinated last year. The cats were not vaccinated last year.

   _____

10. That man does not want to skate right now. His sisters do not want to skate now.

   _____

Chapter Four Supplement

SENTENCE PATTERNS FOR CONTRAST PARAGRAPHS

Four Patterns for Topic Sentences

The topic sentence patterns below introduce only the topics and the controlling idea (differences) in sentences of contrast. You can add more information, such as a general statement, to your topic sentence. Each example is followed by an exercise. Write topic sentences using the sample sentence pattern above each exercise. Follow the examples. Add a general statement to each sentence.

● Pattern #1

There are some amazing differences between Venus and Mercury.

THERE ARE   (#)   [ADJ.]   DIFFERENCES   BETWEEN   X   AND   Y.

Exercise S4.1

Examples

Venus / Mercury

Although they are both planets in our solar system, there are some amazing

differences between Venus and Mercury.

1. television / radio

_____

2. an ocean / a sea

_____

● Pattern #2

X and Y **(be)** *different in* **(#) [adj.]** *ways.*

X **(be)** *different from Y in* **(#) [adj.]** *ways.*

Examples

Rhinos and hippos are different in three important ways.

X   AND   Y   (BE)   DIFFERENT IN   (#)   [ADJECTIVE]   WAYS.

Coffee is different from tea in three   ways.

X   (BE)   DIFFERENT FROM   Y   IN   (#)   [ADJ.]   WAYS.

Exercise S4.2

Examples

rhinos / hippos

Although they are similar to each other in physical appearance and size,

rhinos and hippos are different in three important ways.

coffee / tea

Many believe that coffee and tea have the same effect on the body, but in fact

coffee is different from tea in three important ways.

1. a smile / a frown

_____

2. socialism / capitalism

_____

3. (my two best friends)

_____

Pattern #3

X and Y (be) ***different with respect to*** *[noun phrase].*
X (be) ***different from*** *Y* ***with respect to*** *[noun phrase].*

Examples

Dogs and wolves are different with respect to their physical appearance.
   X   AND   Y   (BE)   DIFFERENT WITH RESPECT TO   [NOUN PHRASE].

Dogs are different from wolves with respect to their physical appearance.
   X   (BE)   DIFFERENT FROM   Y   WITH RESPECT TO   [NOUN PHRASE].

Exercise S4.3

Examples

dogs / wolves (physical appearance)

<u>They are members of the same genus, but if you look closely, you can see that</u>

<u>dogs and wolves are quite different with respect to their physical appearance.</u>

<u>Although it is difficult to see at first glance, dogs are different from wolves with</u>

<u>respect to their physical appearance.</u>

1. a poem / a short story (literary style)

   _____

2. Venezuela / Brazil (natural resources)

   _____

Pattern #4

X ***differ(s) from*** *Y* ***in*** *(#) [adjective]* ***ways.***
X ***contrast(s) with*** *Y* ***in*** *(#) [adjective]* ***ways.***

Examples

Bobcats differ from cougars in three   ways.
   X   DIFFER(S) FROM   Y   IN   (#)   [ADJ.]   WAYS.

Tropical climates contrast with subtropical climates in three important ways.
   X   CONTRAST(S) WITH   Y   IN   (#)   [ADJ.]   WAYS.

Exercise S4.4

Example

bobcats / cougars

They are members of the cat family, but you can easily see that bobcats differ from cougars in three obvious ways.

tropical climates / subtropical climates

In Venezuela, you can find tropical as well as subtropical climates, and although they might feel similarly hot and humid, the tropical climate contrasts with the subtropical in three important ways.

1. Africa / Asia

2. my favorite actor / my favorite actress

3. a monarchy / a dictatorship

4. a dream / a nightmare

Exercise S4.5 With a classmate, rewrite the following boring topic sentences using each one of the sentence patterns from the previous explanation. Add an adjective to each of the sentences to make them more interesting.

1. A mayor is different from a governor.

2. Roller skating and ice skating are different.

_____

3. A pistol is different from a rifle.

_____

Exercise S4.6

Part 1 With a partner, list five possible topics for a contrast paragraph. Be sure that the topics you choose are interesting to both of you.

Example

    differences between computer software and computer hardware _____

1. _____
2. _____
3. _____
4. _____
5. _____

Part 2 Write one topic sentence for each of the topics. Use a different topic sentence pattern for each of the sentences. Add a general statement to each topic sentence.

1. _____
2. _____
3. _____
4. _____
5. _____

Two Patterns for Introducing the Main Support (the Point of the Comparison)

Pattern #1

(transition), *X (be) different from Y with respect to* [noun phrase].

(transition), *X contrasts with Y with respect to* [noun phrase].

(transition), *X differs from Y with respect to* [noun phrase].

Examples

Furthermore, John is different from Tony with respect to personality.
(TRANSITION),   X (BE) DIFFERENT FROM   Y   WITH RESPECT TO [NOUN PHRASE].

In addition, John contrasts with Tony with respect to personality.
(TRANSITION),   X   CONTRASTS WITH   Y   WITH RESPECT TO [NOUN PHRASE].

Furthermore, John differs from Tony with respect to personality.
(TRANSITION),   X   DIFFERS FROM   Y   WITH RESPECT TO [NOUN PHRASE].

Exercise S4.7 Sit with a partner. Discuss the following topics, and then write sentences of contrast using the sentence pattern above and the words in parentheses. Use the given transition words or expressions in the sentence. Use different information for each sentence.

Example

the most famous politician in my country / the most famous politician in my partner's country

    a. (For example…contrast with…with respect to)

        For example, President Gomez contrasts with General Sanchez with

        respect to the types of social programs they support.

1. the most famous politician in my country / the most famous politician in my partner's country

    a. (For example…contrast with…with respect to)

        _____

        _____

b. (also...differ from...with respect to)

_____

_____

2. my hometown / my partner's hometown

a. (In addition...contrast with...with respect to)

_____

_____

b. (Furthermore...be different from...with respect to)

_____

_____

Pattern #2

X and Y [verb] *different* [noun phrase].

Example

My best friends, Tom and Mark, also plan to have very different lifestyles after graduation.
            X AND Y   [VERB]   DIFFERENT   [NOUN PHRASE].

Exercise S4.8 With a classmate, write topic sentences using the sentence pattern above and the topics in parentheses. Do not use *have* or *be* as the main verb in these sentences. Use the given transition words or expressions in the sentence. Add a general statement to each sentence.

1. (moreover...Professor Hanks...Professor Martin...different kinds of exams)

_____

_____

2. (also...oranges...apples...climates)

_____

_____

3. (furthermore...oceans...lakes...kinds of fish)

_____

_____

Six Patterns for Secondary Support (the Contrast Itself)

● Pattern #1

Unlike X, [adjective clause], (complete sentence about Y).

Example

Unlike Arnold, who enjoys skiing and jogging, Juan prefers skating and surfing.
UNLIKE X,   [ADJ. CLAUSE],[1]   (COMPLETE SENTENCE ABOUT Y).

Exercise S4.9 With a classmate, write sentences using the sentence pattern above and the topics given.

Example

my partner / myself

Unlike my partner, who enjoys skiing and surfing during her vacations, I like

to travel to foreign countries and go to concerts.

1. the leader of my country / the leader of my partner's country

_____

2. my partner / myself

_____

---

1 See the Chapter Three Supplement to review adjective clauses.

Pattern #2

> *While* [dependent clause], [independent clause].
>
> [independent clause], *whereas* [dependent clause].

Examples

While some people enjoy visiting museums, I would rather go to the zoo.
WHILE   [DEPENDENT CLAUSE],   [INDEPENDENT CLAUSE].

Jack was found innocent of the crime, whereas his partner was convicted.
          [INDEPENDENT CLAUSE],   WHEREAS   [DEPENDENT CLAUSE].

Note that *while* and *whereas* are subordinating conjunctions, but they have a comma in front of them even if they are in the second part of the sentence.

Exercise S4.10 With a classmate, write sentences using the sentence pattern above and the topics given. If *when* or *while* is capitalized, use it at the beginning of the sentence. If the word has a small letter, use it in the middle of the sentence.

Example

my partner's language / my language

a. (While)

While Spanish has only five vowel sounds, English has more than ten

vowel sounds.

b. (while)

Spanish has only five vowel sounds, while English has more than ten

vowel sounds.

1. my partner's native country / my native country

a. (while)

_____

b. (Whereas)

_____

2. (the government in my partner's country / the government in my own country

   a. (Whereas)

   _____

   b. (whereas)

   _____

● Pattern #3

_X_ (be) _different from Y in that_ [independent clause].

Example

John is different from Mary in that John is shy, but Mary is outgoing.
X   (BE)   DIFFERENT FROM   Y   IN THAT   [INDEPENDENT CLAUSE].

Exercise S4.11 With a classmate, write sentences using the sentence pattern above and the topics given. Make sure to write an independent clause (complete sentence) after _in that._ The sentence must mention both of your topics and the different characteristics of each one.

Example

   your favorite actor / your partner's favorite actor

     Tom Cruise is different from Charles Bronson in that Cruise is young and popular

     among the younger generations, while Bronson is middle-aged and popular

     among older people.

1. your favorite salad / your partner's favorite salad

   _____

   _____

2. (two classmates besides yourselves)

   _____

   _____

3. the climate in your country / the climate in your partner's country

_____

_____

● **Pattern #4**

[independent clause]; *on the other hand,* **[independent clause].**
[independent clause]. *However,* **[independent clause].**
[independent clause]. [Subject], *on the other hand,* **[rest of clause].**

Examples

That candidate is in favor of welfare programs; on the other hand, this candidate is not.
     [INDEPENDENT CLAUSE];   ON THE OTHER HAND,   [INDEPENDENT CLAUSE].

That candidate is in favor of welfare programs. However, this candidate is not.
     [INDEPENDENT CLAUSE].   HOWEVER,   [INDEPENDENT CLAUSE].

That candidate is in favor of welfare programs. This candidate, on the other hand, is not.
     [INDEPENDENT CLAUSE].   [SUBJECT],   ON THE OTHER HAND,   [REST OF CLAUSE].

Exercise 4.12 With a classmate, write sentences using the sentence patterns above and the topics given.

1. my favorite fruit / my partner's favorite fruit

    a. (in contrast)

_____

    b. (on the other hand)

_____

    c. (however)

_____

● Pattern #5

> **[independent clause]**, *but* **[independent clause]**.
> **[independent clause]**, *yet* **[independent clause]**.

Examples

Max is a respected professional, but his brother is a bum.
    [INDEPENDENT CLAUSE],   BUT   [INDEPENDENT CLAUSE].

Max is a respected professional, yet his brother is a bum.
    [INDEPENDENT CLAUSE],   YET   [INDEPENDENT CLAUSE].

Exercise S4.13 With a classmate, write sentences using the sentence pattern above and the topics given.

1. speaking English / writing English

    _____

2. traveling by bus / traveling by airplane

    _____

● Pattern #6 Comparatives

Examples

Max   is   taller than John.
 X   [LINKING VERB]   [ADJ. + -ER]   THAN Y.

James   is   more serious than Jean.
 X   [LINKING VERB]   MORE [ADJ.]   THAN Y.

Max has   a   taller   brother than John.
 X   [VERB] (A/AN) [ADJ. + -ER]   [NOUN]   THAN Y.

James learned   a more difficult lesson than Jean.
  X   [VERB] (A/AN) MORE [ADJ.]   [NOUN]   THAN Y.

Rules for adjectives:

- When an adjective has only one syllable, add -er to the adjective for the comparative.

- When an adjective has three syllables, use *more* and the adjective for the comparative.

- When an adjective has two syllables, remember two rules:

   1. If the adjective ends in consonant + *y,* add -er to the adjective for the comparative.

   2. For most adjectives that do not end in *y* use *more* and the adjective for the comparative.

      pretty → prettier   handsome → **more** handsome

Rules for spelling -*er* adjectives:

- Drop a silent *e* before adding -er.

- When an adjective that has only one syllable ends with the combination of consonant + vowel + consonant (c v c), you must double the last consonant before you add -er (exceptions are *w, y, x*).

Double *cvc* endings:

fat → fatter   thin → thinner
C V C   C V C

No double endings:

nice → nicer   blue → bluer
V C V   C C V

Exceptions (*w, y, x*):

slow → slower   grey → greyer   lax → laxer

Exercise S4.14 With a partner, write comparative sentences using the sentence patterns above and the topics given.

1. a baseball / a basketball (big)

_____

_____

2. an orange / a grapefruit (delicious)

_____

_____

3. a car / a truck (slow)

_____

_____

4. studying / playing (worthwhile)

_____

_____

5. geography / algebra (easy)

_____

_____

Sentence Pattern for the Conclusion: Superlative Adjectives

When your purpose in writing a contrast paragraph is to show that one thing is better than another, the conclusion frequently uses a superlative adjective. Study the charts and explanations below, and then sit with a partner to do the exercises that follow.

• Pattern #1 Superlatives

Examples

Max   is   the   tallest   brother   of the three.
X   [VERB]   THE   [ADJ. + -EST]   [NOUN]   OF [NOUN PHRASE].

James learned the most difficult lesson in that book very quickly.
X   [VERB]   THE MOST   [ADJ.]   [NOUN]   IN   [NOUN PHRASE].

Rules for adjectives:

- When an adjective has only one syllable, use *the* and add *-est* to the adjective for the superlative.

- When an adjective has three syllables, use *the most* and the adjective for the superlative.

- When an adjective has two syllables, remember two rules:

    1. If the adjective ends in consonant + *y,* add *-est* to the adjective for the superlative.

    2. For most adjectives that do not end in *y* use *the most* and the adjective for the superlative.

        pretty → prettiest   handsome → most handsome

Rules for spelling *-est* adjectives:

- Drop a silent *e* before adding *-est.*

- When an adjective that has only one syllable ends with the combination of consonant + vowel + consonant (c v c), you must double the last consonant before you add *-est* (exceptions are *w, y, x).*

Double *cvc* endings:

fat → fattest   thin → thinnest
c v c   c v c

No double endings:

nice → nicest   blue → bluest
v c v   c c v

Exceptions *(w, y, x)*:

slow → slowest   grey → greyest   lax → laxest

Exercise 4.15 Compare the following. Use comparatives for the first two elements and then a superlative for all three items.

1. a dog / a cat / a parakeet

    a. _____

    b. _____

2. running / walking / swimming

   a. _____

   b. _____

3. coffee / tea / milk

   a. _____

   b. _____

Chapter Five Supplement

THE PASSIVE VOICE: INTRODUCTION

To use the passive voice, you must know how to:

1. Locate a subject in a sentence.

2. Identify transitive and intransitive verbs (find the objects in a sentence).

3. Write past participles of irregular (and regular) verbs.[1]

4. Identify the tenses of verbs in active sentences.

5. Conjugate the verb *be*.

Identifying the Subject of a Sentence

To find the subject in a sentence, look for the verb (the action) and ask, "Who or what is performing this action?" The answer to this question will show you the subject of the verb.

Example

Debbie speaks five language? **Who** speaks? **Subject = "Debbie"**

Exercise S5.1   Circle the subjects in the following sentences:

1. Pink is my daughter's favorite color.

2. When will you visit them?

3. Next week, the telephone company will send the bill.

4. There are many people in this class.

5. This recording on the telephone is very annoying.

---

1 For irregular past participles, see Appendix Three.

6. Her social security number is 000-00-1234.

7. Sergio helped sign up the girls for medical insurance.

8. The thunder and lightning seemed to be closer than a mile from the house.

9. In the morning, the weather forecaster said that the weekend weather was going to be beautiful.

10. In this neighborhood, you can hear dogs barking all night long.

Identifying Transitive and Intransitive Verbs

Some verbs must have a direct object to be complete. Others cannot have a direct object. It is important to know the difference between these two kinds of verbs because intransitive verbs can NOT be written in the passive voice.

Examples

I	gave	the ball	to the dog.
	TRANSITIVE VERB	DIRECT OBJECT	INDIRECT OBJECT

I	slept	until 9:00.
	INTRANSITIVE VERB	(NO OBJECT POSSIBLE)

The following sentences are wrong.

I sent. **(This is not a complete sentence.)**

I slept the baby. **(This is not a correct sentence.)**

Identifying Direct Objects

To find the direct object in a sentence, ask the following informal question based on your sentence:

[Subject] [verb] WHAT or WHOM?

Example

I saw **you** yesterday in the park. I saw **whom?** **Direct object = "you"**

Exercise S5.2 Sit with a partner and write one complete sentence for each of the following words. Then exchange papers with another pair of students in the class and circle the direct object in each of their sentences. Return the papers to the original owners and correct their errors. Tell the other pair how they did on your sentences, and explain any errors to them.

1. send _____ .

2. write _____ .

3. pass _____ .

4. throw _____ .

5. take _____ .

6. buy _____ .

7. mail _____ .

8. erase _____ .

9. build _____ .

10. wash _____ .

Identifying Indirect Objects

To find the indirect object in a sentence, ask the following informal question based on your sentence:

[Subject] [verb] [direct object] + to WHOM?

Example

I gave **you** my book.

I	gave	my book	**TO**	**WHOM?**	**Indirect object = "you"**
SUBJECT	VERB	DIRECT OBJECT	TO	WHOM?	

You can find the indirect object in two different places in a sentence. It may be after or before the direct object. If the indirect object is before the direct object, there is no "to" in front of it. If it is after the direct object, there is "to" in front of it.

Example

	INDIRECT OBJECT NO "TO"	DIRECT OBJECT
I gave	**you**	a note.

	DIRECT OBJECT	INDIRECT OBJECT
I gave	a note	**to you.**

Exercise S5.3 With your partner, add an indirect object to each of the following sentences. Be careful with "to"!

1. Our instructor gave a bad grade _____ on the last test.

2. Our instructor gave _____ a bad grade on the last test.

3. Robert brought _____ a present.

4. Robert brought a present _____ .

5. Mr. Simpson brought a bouquet of roses _____ for their anniversary.

6. Mr. Simpson brought _____ a bouquet of roses for their anniversary.

Identifying Verb Tenses

When you want to change a sentence from active voice to passive voice, you have to know the tense of the main verb, because in the passive voice, you will use that same tense for the verb *be*.

Sentence in Active Voice	Tenses of Main Verb	Conjugation of *be*	Past Participle	Sentence in Passive Voice
She *opens* the mail.	simple present	is / am / are	opened	The mail *is opened*.
She *opened* the mail.	simple past	was / were	opened	The mail *was opened*.
She *will open* the mail.	simple future	will be	opened	The mail *will be opened*.
She *is opening* the mail.	present progressive	is being	opened	The mail *is being opened*.
She *was opening* the mail	past progressive	was being	opened	The mail *was being opened*.
She *has opened* the mail.	present perfect	has been	opened	The mail *has been opened*
She *had opened* the mail.	past perfect	had been	opened	The mail *had been opened*.
She *will have opened* the mail	future perfect	will have been	opened	The mail *will have been opened*.
She *can open* the mail.	modal **can**	can be	opened	The mail *can be opened*.
She *could open* the mail.	modal **could**	could be	opened	The mail *could be opened*.
She *would open* the mail.	modal **would**	would be	opened	The mail *would be opened*.
She *may open* the mail.	modal **may**	may be	opened	The mail *may be opened*.
She *might open* the mail.	modal **might**	might be	opened	The mail *might be opened*.

Sentence in Active Voice	Tenses of Main Verb	Conjugation of *be*	Past Participle	Sentence in Passive Voice
She *should open* the mail.	modal **should**	should be	opened	The mail *should be opened.*
She *will be opening* the mail.	future progressive			(passive voice not possible)
She *has been opening* the mail.	present perfect progressive			(passive voice not possible)
She *had been opening* the mail.	past perfect progressive			(passive voice not possible)
She *will have been opening* the mail.	future perfect progressive			(passive voice not possible)

Exercise S5.4 Name the tense of the main verb in each of the following sentences.

Example

    We are studying this tomorrow. _present progressive (or present continuous)_

1. I **have gone** there several times. _____

2. We **were driving** for seven hours in the rain. _____

3. Nguyen **won't be** here until tomorrow. _____

4. You **can do** it later. _____

5. They'**re** here. _____

6. We **had finished** it by the time they **arrived.** _____ ;

    _____

7. We **will have left** by the time they arrive. _____

8. Sam **is leaving** now. _____

9. They **considered** the idea. _____

10. Jane can write **French.** _____

Which of the above sentences have intransitive verbs? (Hint: There are six.)

    _____

Can the sentences with intransitive verbs be passive? _____

USING THE PASSIVE VOICE

Now you are ready to write passive sentences. To change a sentence from active voice to passive voice, follow these three steps:

Step #1 The object (direct or indirect) of the active voice sentence is the subject of the passive sentence. This means that if the verb does not have a direct object, you cannot put it into the passive voice. There is no possible subject for a passive sentence.

DIRECT
OBJECT

She opens **the mail.**

The mail is opened (by her).

SUBJECT

Step #2 The main verb of the active sentence becomes a passive verb. The passive verb consists of TWO verbs: the verb *be*, which is conjugated in the same tense as the main verb in the active sentence, and the past participle form of the main verb from the active sentence.

MAIN VERB
(PRESENT TENSE)

She **opens** the mail.

The mail **is** **opened** (by her).

BE   PAST
(PRESENT   PARTICIPLE
TENSE)   OF MAIN VERB

Step #3 The subject of the active sentence is often optional in the passive voice. It is called "the agent," and if you do not need to mention it, don't. You especially do not need to mention the agent if it is not a specific person or specific people.

SUBJECT

She opens the mail.

The mail is opened (by her).

(AGENT)

Examples

Active Voice	Passive Voice
My mother bore me in Eureka, California.	I was born in Eureka, California.
Construction workers built this college ten years ago.	This college was built ten years ago.
They did not build this college last year.	This college wasn't built last year.
A person uses special cameras to take underwater pictures.	Special cameras are used to take underwater pictures.
Do you make antique tables here? (Yes, we do.)	Are antique tables made here? (Yes, they are.)

We don't make antique tables here.	Antique tables are not made here.
People grow delicious coffee in Colombia.	Delicious coffee is grown in Colombia.
People do not grow good coffee in Florida.	Good coffee is not grown in Florida.
I broke your window with a ball.	Your window was broken by a ball.
My husband ran over your dog this morning.	Your dog was run over this morning.

In the active voice, it is easy to see who performs the action in the sentence: the subject of the sentence. In the active voice, the subject is an important element in the sentence. Sometimes, however, you do not want to emphasize the performer of the action. Maybe the performer of the action is not a specific person, or maybe you want your audience to focus on the object of the sentence. You might want to hide the identity of the performer of the action. In this case, the passive voice allows your sentence to focus on the object of the sentence or on the action itself. It is not even necessary, in many cases, to mention the performer of the action. The following sentences sound silly:

I was borne in Eureka, California **by my mother.**

This college was built ten years ago **by construction workers.**

Delicious coffee is grown in Colombia **by people.**

And this sentence would not let the performer of the action remain anonymous:

Your window was broken **by me** with a ball.

A passive sentence is a complete sentence even when you do not mention the performer of the action. When you change a sentence from active voice to passive voice, the subject of the passive sentence is the former direct or indirect object of the active sentence.

Active: John didn't give a book to Mary.

Passive: 1. Mary wasn't given a book. **(indirect object as subject)**

2. A book wasn't given to Mary. **(direct object as subject)**

Active: They sent a letter to his father.

Passive: 1. His father was sent a letter. **(indirect object as subject)**

2. A letter was sent to his father. **(direct object as subject)**

Exercises S5.5 Change the **boldfaced** phrases and sentences in the following paragraphs from active to passive voice in the spaces below.

    The coffee plant is an evergreen shrub (genus Coffea of the madder family) (1) **that people grow** in rich soil of countries with hot moist climates. After (2) **people grow the coffee plants,** which take several years to mature, (3) **people harvest, clean, and roast the seeds.** (4) **The heat brings out the delicious aroma and flavor of the coffee bean.** (5) **People do not grind the beans** on the plantations where they grow the beans. (6) **They export the beans,** and the (7) **companies that purchase the beans grind them and package them.** (8) **You can buy ground coffee or whole coffee beans in most stores.**

1. _____

2. _____

3. _____

4. _____

5. _____

6. _____

7. _____

8. _____

    The term *kosher* applies to food that is prepared according to Jewish dietary laws. (1) **People have explained the origins of Jewish dietary laws and customs** as hygienic, folkloric, ethical, psychological, and aesthetic. (2) **Jews consider animals that chew their cud and have cloven hooves, such as cows and sheep, to be kosher.** (3) **Jews also consider fish that have scales and fins to be kosher.** It is not kosher to drink milk with meat or poultry, or to cook milk in any meat or poultry dish.

1. _____

2. _____

3. _____

    As you do the paragraphs in Chapters 5 and 6 of this text, use the passive voice in the assignments.

Chapter Six Supplement

REDUCED ADJECTIVE CLAUSES (ADJECTIVE PHRASES)

Introduction: "Less Is More"

As you progress to more advanced writing classes, your teachers will tell you to avoid "wordiness." Communicate your message without "flowery" writing. Look at the difference between these sentences. One is "wordy"; the other is concise. Which is easier to read? A good rule to remember when writing is "less is more." What do you think "less is more" means?

1. The person who is talking to the man who is standing on the corner is a friend of my brother, whose name is John.

2. The person talking to the man on the corner is a friend of my brother, John.

In this supplement you will learn to reduce adjective clauses to adjective phrases. This is important when writing the definition exercises in Chapter 6 because it allows you to put more information into your definition sentences without sounding too "wordy." First, let's look at the difference between a **clause** and a **phrase.**

● What Is a Clause?

A **clause** is a group of words that contains at least a subject and a verb. It is not always a complete sentence. Some clauses are dependent or subordinate clauses (see the Appendix 2 for subordinate clauses):

They will do it later.   People enjoy her books.
                (INDEPENDENT CLAUSES)

When I was little   After you eat lunch
(DEPENDENT CLAUSES = NOT COMPLETE SENTENCES)

Sometimes clauses are complete sentences:

He arrived to class on time.   The movie was good.

• What Is a Phrase?

A **phrase** is a group of words that does not contain a subject and a verb. It is never a complete sentence:

in the morning   going to the beach   much later than that

Exercise S6.1   Write *C* in front of the clauses and *P* in front of the phrases.

___   1. The student next to John.

___   2. The car stopped.

___   3. When he was a very small boy.

___   4. We went to see a movie.

___   5. In the morning or in the afternoon.

In the Chapter 2 Supplement you learned to write adjective clauses. In this lesson you will learn to reduce an adjective clause to an adjective phrase. If you are not sure about how to write adjective clauses, you need to review that Supplement before continuing this one.

It is important to understand that only adjective clauses with subject pronouns can be made into adjective phrases. Therefore, to change an adjective clause into an adjective phrase, you must know the difference between a subject pronoun and an object pronoun in the adjective clause.

- • How can you tell if a relative pronoun is an **object** pronoun? **It is followed by a subject and then a verb.**

- • How can you tell if a relative pronoun is a **subject** pronoun? **It is followed directly by a verb.**

The house **which**   we   were   going to buy burned down.

[OBJECT]   SUBJECT   VERB
RELATIVE PRONOUN

The house **which** burned down was not insured.

[SUBJECT]　　VERB
RELATIVE PRONOUN

Exercise S6.2 <u>Underline</u> the subject pronouns and (circle) the object pronouns in the adjective clauses in the following sentences.

1. The student whom you spoke to yesterday told me that you were sick.

2. The student who was talking to you yesterday told me that you were sick.

3. Ernie, whom everyone likes, is moving to North Carolina.

4. Ernie, who is moving to North Carolina, is one of the most popular people in our school.

5. The computer lab, which Midge directs, is very busy this time of the semester.

6. The computer lab, which is in Building 6, is very busy this time of the semester.

7. Do you know the man who is sitting in the corner?

8. Do you know the man that John is talking about?

9. The computer which broke down last week has been repaired.

10. The computer which you broke last week has been repaired.

Changing Adjective Clauses to Adjective Phrases

There are two ways in which an adjective clause can become an adjective phrase.

● **#1**

When the verb *be* is in the adjective clause and the relative pronoun is the **subject** of the adjective clause, you can reduce the clause to a phrase by eliminating the relative pronoun and *be*.

In the sentences below, the relative pronouns *(who* and *which)* are **subject** pronouns and the verb in the adjective clause is *be*. Notice that if the adjective clause require commas, the adjective phrase also requires commas.

a. The student **who is laughing at Juan** is being rude.

b. The student ~~**who is**~~ **laughing at Juan** is being rude.

a. Mary, **who is a girl with a terrific sense of humor,** makes our class enjoyable.

b. Mary, ~~**who is**~~ **a girl with a terrific sense of humor,** makes our class enjoyable.

a. The lesson **which is now being studied by this class** is not difficult.

b. The lesson ~~**which is**~~ **now being studied by this class** is not difficult.

Exercise S6.3 Change the adjective clauses in the following sentences to adjective phrases. Some of the sentences have more than one adjective clause.

1. The teacher who was telling you to be quiet was getting angry.

   _____

2. The car which was following us looked like it was having engine problems.

   _____

3. Dr. McCabe, who was the president of the college, quit his job last year.

   _____

4. The sun, which is visible only during the day, consists of gas that is held together by its own gravity.

   _____

   _____

5. The heart, which is the organ that is pumping blood to all parts of its body, is transparent.

   _____

   _____

6. A volcano, which is an opening in the crust of the earth, can be active, dormant, or extinct.

   _____

   _____

7. Rhonda, who is the IBM trainer at the college, lectures at conferences which are all over the country.

_____

_____

8. Jenny, who is a dancer and an author, teaches modern dance at MacMillan Middle School.

_____

_____

9. June, which is the beginning of hurricane season in the southeast of the United States, is a hot and humid month.

_____

_____

10. Chicken pox, which is a childhood disease, is highly contagious.

_____

Exercise S6.4 Change the adjective phrases in the following sentences to adjective clauses. Some of the sentences have more than one adjective phrase.

1. The person you are looking for is in the car by the gymnasium.

_____

2. The doctor talking on the phone is going to the cafeteria on the third floor after her shift.

_____

_____

3. Leslie, the best football player in our school, is dating Michelle, the most popular cheerleader.

_____

_____

4. Austin, the capital of Texas, is one of the most beautiful cities in the United States.

_____

5. The dog running in the street belongs to the people living in the blue house.

_____

● #2

If the adjective clause does not have *be*, it is sometimes possible to omit the subject pronoun and change the verb to its *-ing* form to create an adjective phrase. But be careful. Frequently, using this structure will cause confusion if the main verb in the adjective clause is an action verb. It can make a simple present tense sound like a present continuous tense.

Examples

OK	Anyone who speaks French can do it.	Anyone speaking French can do it.
NO	John, who speaks French, understands this.	John, speaking French, understands this. (IT SOUNDS LIKE JOHN IS SPEAKING FRENCH AT THIS MOMENT.)

With nonaction verbs (such as *know, like, think*) there is no confusion because the verbs are not used in the present continuous form.

OK	Any one **who knows** French can do it.	Anyone **knowing** French can do it.
OK	A person **who knows** French can do it.	A person **knowing** French can do it.
OK	John, **who knows** French, can do it.	John, **knowing** French, can do it.
OK	People **who know** French can do it.	People **knowing** French can do it.
OK	Everyone **who knows** French can do it.	Everyone **knowing** French can do it.

The Yurok Indians **who lived** in Northern California caught surf fish at Luffenholtz.

The Yurok Indians **living** in Northern California caught surf fish at Luffenholtz.

The people **who think** he will win the elections are mistaken.

The people **thinking** he will win the elections are mistaken.

Many people **who want** to live to an old age still believe that we should develop more nuclear weapons.

Many people **wanting** to live to an old age still believe that we should develop more nuclear weapons.

Exercise S6.5 Change the adjective clauses in these sentences into adjective phrases where possible.

1. W.E.B. Du Bois, who was a black American civil rights leader and author, cofounded the National Negro Committee in 1910.

   _____

   _____

   _____

2. Exeter, which is the capital of Devonshire in England, has many historic sites such as the Norman Cathedral.

   _____

   _____

3. One of the most famous American bank robbers was John Dillinger, who killed 16 people.

   _____

   _____

4. Thon Buri, which is part of metropolitan Bangkok, is an industrial city.

   _____

   _____

5. Ludmila, who works in the school cafeteria, likes to vacation in Vladivostok, which is a city on the Sea of Japan.

   _____

   _____

6. Qiqihar, which is an industrial city in northeast China, is one of the coldest cities in China in the winter.

   _____

   _____

7. Guyana, which was declared an independent republic in 1970, has a hot and humid climate.

_____

_____

8. Selma Lagerlöf, who was the first woman to receive the Nobel Prize in literature, was born in Sweden in 1858.

_____

_____

9. Immanuel Kant, who was a German philosopher, was one of the most important figures in the history of metaphysics, which is the branch of philosophy concerned with the nature of existence.

_____

_____

_____

10. Antarctica, which Professor James visited last year, consists of two major regions: West Antarctica, which includes the Antarctic Peninsula, and East Antarctica, which is a continental shield area.

_____

_____

_____

_____

appendix
one

General Punctuation Rules

END PUNCTUATION

1. Use a period to end a statement or a command.

    The sun is shining today[.]   Go go bed[.]

2. Use a question mark to end a question.

    Where are you going[?]   You are not happy, are you[?]

3. Use an exclamation point to end a sentence that expresses strong emotion.

    Stop[!]   You are going the wrong direction[!]   Good grief[!]

COMMA

1. Use a comma before a coordinator that connects two complete sentences.

    She studies a lot, yet she fails her tests.

    We went inside, but they stayed outside in the rain.

    But don't use a comma if the sentences are not complete.

    The teacher came in and sat down at the desk.

    We usually travel to California or to Oregon in the summer.

2. Use a comma between items in a series.

    She loves to play tennis, go bowling, and ride horses.

3. Use a comma after the dependent clause if it is first in the sentence.[1]

   Because you came early, we will have time to do two of the lessons.

   But don't use a comma if the dependent clause comes after the independent clause.

   We will have time to do two of the lessons because you came early.

4. Use a comma after transitional words and expressions (and use a period or semi-colon in front of them).

   I hear the phone ringing; however, I am too busy to answer it.

   You need to see a dentist. Nevertheless, you refuse to make the appointment.

5. Use a comma in front of expressions like "especially," "such as," "namely," or "for example."

   This college has students from all over the world, especially from South America.

   There are many sports one can practice in the winter in Canada, such as skiing and ice skating.

   But you can use a colon to introduce a list or an explanation.

   There are three French students in our class: Janine, Pierre, and Etienne.

   This class has one outstanding feature: the modern technology used by the teacher.

6. Use a comma after a long introductory clause or phrase.

   After dinner last Sunday evening, we took a walk in the park.

   In the evenings, we like to watch the sun setting over the ocean.

7. Use a comma to separate an appositive from the rest of the sentence.

   Professor James, her English teacher, gave her this book to read.

   My best friend, Mary Smith, lives in Tampa.

8. Use a comma to separate nonrestrictive relative clauses from the rest of the sentence. A relative clause is nonrestrictive if the information in the clause is not needed to identify the subject of the sentence.

   Jarvis, who was elected chairperson, is from New York.
   (THE INFORMATION IN THE RELATIVE CLAUSE IS NOT NEEDED TO EXPLAIN "WHICH JARVIS.")

   The man who was elected chairperson is from New York.
   (THE INFORMATION IN THE RELATIVE CLAUSE IS NEEDED TO EXPLAIN "WHICH MAN.")

---

1 The exceptions to this rule are the subordinators that show a contrast or surprise: though, although, whereas, while.

9. Use commas with direct address.

   Mother, can you please come here for a second?

   John, please sit down and be still.

10. Use a comma after "yes" and "no" in answers.

    Yes, I will go with you.

    No, I will be busy at that time.

11. Use a comma in direct quotations.

    John asked, "Will the test be on Friday?"

    The teacher responded, "No, it will be next Wednesday, John."

12. Use a comma with dates, addresses, page references, measurements, and similar information.

    She was born on January 15, 1954, in a small town in California.

    Luis moved, and his new address is 12234 Kendall Drive, Miami, Florida.

    Julie is five feet, two inches tall.

    Page 3, Section 2 needs to be revised.

13. Use a comma with coordinate adjectives. Coordinate adjectives are adjectives whose location in the sentence can be changed without changing the meaning of the sentence.

    She has a strange, exotic smile.

    This is a dreary, spooky road.

14. Use a comma between contrasting expressions.

    You must study, not play.

    This is the end, not the beginning.

SEMICOLON

1. Use a semicolon between two complete sentences that are closely related in meaning.

   Some teachers give objective test items; others prefer essay questions.

   Miami has a wonderful climate; many tourists go there in the winter.

APOSTROPHE

1. Use an apostrophe for a contraction.

   We'd better go. **(We HAD better go.)**

   We'd rather not do this now. **(We WOULD rather not do this now.)**

2. Use an apostrophe to show possession in a noun.

   Singular: Mary's mother.

   The boy's book. **(The book belongs to one boy.)**

   Plural: The boys' bathroom. **(The bathroom belongs to more than one boy.)**

   The men's bathroom. **(The bathroom belongs to more than one man.)**

appendix
two

Connecting Words

COORDINATING CONJUNCTIONS

Coordinating Conjunctions
and   but   yet   so   for   or   nor

Coordinating conjunctions can connect complete sentences or parts of sentences. These conjunctions usually require a comma when they connect two complete sentences, unless the sentences are short, but never use a comma when the coordinator connects only two words or phrases. To connect more than two items in a list, use commas to separate all of the items.

And is used for giving **additional information.** Writers will sometimes use *and* or *but* at the beginning of a sentence, but only to show a sudden or important afterthought. You should not use *and* or *but* to begin a sentence in which you simply want to show additional information *(and)* or a contrast *(but)*.

Examples

Tom is a lawyer, **and** he works at a firm downtown.

I like sugar **and** cream in my coffee.

I like sugar, cream, **and** a little cinnamon in my coffee.

Exercise A2.1   Combine the following sentences with *and*.

1. Leroy enjoys books by M. Crichton. Leroy enjoys books by S. King.

2. We need to buy some sugar. We need to buy some cereal.

_____

3. John left early. Mark left early. Henry left early.

_____

- Use *but* and *yet* to show **contrast, contradiction,** or **surprise.**

Examples

I don't like him, **but** I will go to the dance with him.

This is not fresh bread, **yet** he is buying it anyway. (Yuck!)

Exercise A2.2 Complete the following ideas with *but* and another idea that surprises or contrasts with the first. Use correct punctuation.

1. Somebody is knocking on the door _____ .

2. I studied for the last test _____ .

3. The teacher told us to write in ink _____ .

- Use *so* to show the result of an action.

Examples

I didn't study much for the last exam, **so** I got a bad grade.

Sally is studying medicine, **so** I suppose she wants to be a doctor.

Exercise A2.3 Complete the following sentence with *so*. Use correct punctuation.

1. Somebody is knocking on the door _____ .

2. I studied for the last test _____ .

3. The teacher told us to write in ink _____ .

- Use *for* to show a **reason** or **cause** for an action. Do not use *for* in conversational English speech. It sounds very formal.

Examples

> I have watched all of his movies, **for** he is the best actor I have ever seen.
>
> She believes you, **for** you have always told her the truth.

Exercise A2.4 Complete the following sentence with *for*. Use correct punctuation.

1. Wendall had to go to court _____ .

2. Jeanny failed the course last semester _____ .

3. Nobody could believe him _____ .

- Use *or* to show an **option** or **alternative.**

Examples

> We may go to Europe, **or** we may decide to go to South America.
>
> You may go to the library **or** to the lab to study.
>
> You may go to the library, to the lab, **or** to the cafeteria to study.

Exercise A2.5 Ask a partner to answer the following questions giving options with *or*.
Write your partner's answers on a separate piece of paper.

1. What will you do after you graduate? (give several options)

2. Where would you like to travel? (give several options)

3. What will you do this weekend? (give several options)

- Use *nor* to show a negative option. But BEWARE ! After *nor,* you must reverse the usual order of subject and verb:

Examples

> I don't want to go to the beach. I don't want to go to the park.
>
> I don't want to go to the beach, **nor** **do** **I** **want to go** to the park.
>
> AUXILIARY SUBJECT VERB
>
> John won't go to the beach. I won't go to the beach.
>
> John won't go to the beach, **nor** **will** **I.**
>
> AUXILIARY SUBJECT (NOTHING ELSE NEEDED)

Tim doesn't like the topic of the paper. Tim doesn't like the style of the paper.

Tim doesn't like the topic of the paper, **nor   does   he   like** its style.

AUXILIARY   SUBJECT   VERB

Tim didn't like the topic of the paper. John didn't like the topic of the paper.

Tim didn't like the topic of the paper I wrote, **nor did   John.**

AUXILIARY   SUBJECT   (NOTHING ELSE NEEDED)

Exercise A2.6   Use the following pattern to complete these sentences: *nor* + auxiliary verb (or *be*) + subject.

1. Addis Ababa, the capital of Ethiopia, **does not have** regular addresses,

   _____ have fast-moving local transportation, for only the

   main roads have official names, and the residential areas have twisted street pat-

   terns or only dirt paths.

2. Barranquilla **is not** the capital of Colombia, _____ Cartagena.

3. Timbuktu in Mali **will not** be accessible by car this year, _____

   _____ accessible by bus or train. You will have to go there by camel!

4. You **should not** try to travel the Alaska highway in January, _____

   _____ try to travel it in February or March because the snow is too deep

   and your car could get stuck.

Exercise A2.7   Combine the following words using *nor.*

1. I won't arrive at class on time. John won't arrive at class on time.

   _____

2. I won't arrive at class on time. I won't arrive at work on time.

   _____

3. We shouldn't study tonight. We shouldn't worry about the test.

   _____

4. We shouldn't study tonight. We shouldn't study tomorrow night.

_____

Exercise A2.8 Coordinating Conjunctions Use *and, but, yet, so, for, or,* or *nor* to combine each group of sentences. Eliminate any words that are repeated and/or unnecessary.

Example

The roads are slippery. / The roads are too dangerous.

The roads are too slippery and dangerous.

1. Bad weather causes many traffic problems in Detroit. / It causes schools to close.

_____

2. Snow causes problems for adults in Toronto. / Children love the bad weather. / They love to play in the snow.

_____

3. People do not drive on icy roads. (use *nor*) / People do not ride on icy roads. / The roads are too slippery. / The roads are too dangerous.

_____

4. Children do not have to go to school when it snows a lot in Portland. / Adults do not have to go to work. (use *nor*) / They stay home. / They enjoy their unexpected holiday.

_____

5. Good television commercials use the best actors and actresses. / These commercials take a long time to make. / They are quite expensive.

_____

6. You should return his call soon. / He sounded angry.

_____

7. We realize you have a busy schedule. / Could you please visit this company tomorrow afternoon?

_____

8. You shouldn't fight with your brother. (use *nor*) / You shouldn't call him names.

_____

9. We do not understand the problem. (use *nor*) / We do not understand the proposed solution to the problem.

Subordinating Conjunctions for Chronological Order

● What Is a Clause?

On page 209, you learned about clauses and phrases. Remember that a clause is a group of words that has a subject and a verb. Some clauses are complete sentences:

Samantha left early.   The dog jumped on the visitor.   She is not paid to do that.

Some clauses are not complete sentences:

after you left   in the corner of the room where he stood quietly

A subordinate clause, also called an **adverb clause,** is introduced by a subordinating conjunction which expresses a relationship such as time, place, manner, cause and effect, condition, purpose, or comparison or contrast. A subordinate clause is never a complete sentence by itself. It always needs an independent clause (another complete sentence with a subject and a verb) to complete its meaning.

● Punctuation of Subordinate Clauses

To write a sentence with a subordinate clause, you need to remember two rules for punctuation:

1. If you begin your sentence with the subordinate clause (the sentence that begins with the subordinator), put a comma after the clause.

   When we arrive late⟨,⟩ we cannot see the beginning of the play.

2. If you begin your sentence with the independent clause, you usually[1] do not need a comma after the independent clause.

   We cannot see the beginning of the play **when** we arrive late.

---

1 Subordinators that show contrast, such as *while* and *whereas,* **do** need commas in front of them even when the subordinate clause is not first in the sentence. (The comma reflects the speaker's pause and emphasizes the contrast.)

● Subordinators of Time

In paragraphs of illustration, the body often gives a narration that illustrates the topic sentence's main idea. To show the chronological order of the events in a narrative paragraph, use subordinators such as *when, as soon as, before, after,* and *while.* Do not use the future tense (or the present continuous if it indicates future time) in the subordinate clause.

Examples

Wrong: When you **will come** to class tomorrow **,** you will have a substitute teacher.

Correct: When you **come** to class tomorrow **,** you will have a substitute teacher.

When, once, just as

With *when, once,* and *just as,* the action in the dependent clause (the *when* clause) happens first or at the same time.

- *When* can also mean "every time."

- *Just as* means "at the same instant or moment," and it indicates that the action begins or ends at the moment that action in the independent clause happens.

- *Once* means "immediately after."

Examples

When the plane passed by, I heard a loud noise in the air. **(at that very moment)**

The car stopped **just as** the light turned red. **(at that precise moment)**

Once you understand the rule for punctuation, this is not difficult at all. **(immediately after)**

Exercise A2.9 You do it: Combine these sentences using the subordinator in parentheses.

1. (just as) I closed the door. I remembered that my keys were still in the house.

   _____

2. (once) You will check in at the front desk. You may go to the pool.

   _____

3. (when) You will finish your dinner. You will take your dishes into the kitchen.

   _____

Ask a classmate: "What will you do once you have learned English?"

While, as long as

While and *as long as* have several different meanings. As subordinating conjunctions of time, these words indicate actions that happen simultaneously. The action in the dependent clause can be in the present continuous tense if the action is occurring now, or it can be in the simple present tense (see second example) if the action described in the main clause happens habitually.

- You can also use the simple present tense after *while,* but in this case, the action in the second clause is usually future tense and tells of an **intention.**

- *As long as* can indicate that the actions will happen simultaneously under certain conditions, or it can indicate a consequence.

Examples

While you are watching television **,** she is reading a book.

I am going to go to the office for a dictionary *while* you finish this exercise.

(Both actions are happening at the same time.)

While Ana Maria drives **,** she puts on her makeup.

(Every time she drives, she puts on her makeup.)

As long as you believe that you will fail **,** you will never succeed.

You will never succeed **as long as** you believe you will fail.

(Consequence)

Exercise A2.10   You do it: Combine these sentences using the subordinator in parentheses.

1. (as long as) You continue to turn your work in late. Your grade will not improve.

   _____

2. (while) You are going to chop the onions. I am going to mix the other ingredients.

   _____

Ask a classmate: "What are you doing while you are studying here at this college? (Working? Raising a family?)

Before

With *before,* the action in the subordinate clause occurs SECOND or last. The action in the independent clause happens first. Again remember—you may NOT use future tense in the *before* clause.

> **Wrong: Before** we ~~will~~ go to the store **,** we must go to the bank.

> **Correct: Before** we go to the store, we must go to the bank.

After

When you use *after,* the action that follows *after* occurs FIRST. The action in the independent clause happens second.

Examples

> **After** you wash your hands with antibacterial soap, put on the surgical gloves.

> Decide on the controlling idea **after** you focus your topic.

Exercise A2.11   You do it: Combine these sentences using the subordinator in parentheses. Make sure your sentences are logical.

1. (before) Henry will graduate from the university. He will work for IBM.

   _____

2. (after) Henry will graduate from the university. He will work for IBM.

   _____

3. (before) The students will turn in their paragraphs. The class will end.

   _____

4. (after) The students will turn in their paragraphs. The class will end.

   _____

Ask a classmate:

1. After you arrived in this country, did you feel homesick?

2. Before you traveled to this country for the first time, what did you think you would see here? Were you surprised? Why?

As

As has three meanings. It can indicate time, cause/effect, or manner. When you use *as* to indicate time, it reflects actions that happen simultaneously (at the same time). Do NOT use the future tense (or the present continuous) in clauses that begin with *as* if the sentence indicates time.

Examples

As you grow older, you will learn to appreciate your parents' advice.

It started to rain **as** we arrived at work.

Ask a classmate: "As you learn more and more English, how is your life in this country changing?"

As soon as

With *as soon as,* the action in the dependent clause happens just before another action occurs. You may NOT use the future tense (or the present continuous) in clauses that begin with *as soon as.*

Examples

As soon as you finish, we will go to the concert. **(First you will finish. Then we will go.)**

Put in the corn **as soon as** the water begins to boil. **(First the water begins to boil. Then you put in the corn.)**

Until

Until means "up to that time" or "up to that point." The action in the independent clause stops just as the action or event in the dependent clause occurs.

Examples

I didn't understand the word **until** I looked it up in a dictionary.

I will study this **until** I understand it.

Exercise A2.12   You do it: Combine these sentences using the subordinator in parentheses.

1. (as) English will become easier for you. Life in this country will become easier for you.

_____

_____

2. (as soon as) Joseph will finish his degree in economics. He will work for his father.

_____

_____

3. (until) You can stay in my house. You will find your own apartment.

_____

_____

4. (until) You will learn English better. It will not be easy for you to talk to Americans.

_____

_____

Ask a classmate: "Do you think life is becoming easier for you as you learn English? Are you adapting to this culture?"

Exercise A2.13 Combine these sentences using the subordinator in parentheses. There may be more than one correct answer.

1. (just as) I closed the door. I remembered that my keys were still in the house.

_____

_____

2. (once) You will check in at the front desk. You may go to the pool.

_____

_____

3. (when) You will finish your dinner. You should take your dishes into the kitchen.

_____

_____

4. (as) English will become easier for you. Life in this country will become easier for you.

_____

_____

5. (as soon as) Joseph will finish his degree in economics. He will work for his father.

_____

_____

6. (before) You will move out of your parents' house. You need to find your own apartment.

_____

_____

7. (until) You will learn English better. It might be difficult to travel in the United States.

_____

_____

Ask a classmate:

1. What will you do **once** you have learned English?

2. What are you doing **while** you are studying here at this college? (Working? Raising a family?)

3. **After** you arrived in this country, did you feel homesick?

4. **Before** you traveled to this country for the first time, what did you think you would see here? Were you surprised? Why?

5. Do you think life is becoming easier for you **as** you learn English? Are you adapting to this culture?

Transitional Words and Expressions

Transitional words (conjunctive adverbs) and _transitional expressions_ show relationships between ideas, just as coordinating conjunctions and subordinating conjunctions do. They connect one complete sentence to another complete sentence or one paragraph to another paragraph. In paragraphs, they are often used to indicate the transition (change) from one supporting idea to the next, and they show the logical relation between those ideas.

In paragraphs of illustration, you can use transitional words and expressions to introduce an illustration or example, to give additional information, to signal chronological order, and to conclude. The words you learn here can help you write anecdotes and paragraphs of illustration and examples. You will learn other transitional expressions in future chapters.

Punctuation of Transitional Words and Expressions

1. When you use a transitional word or expression to introduce a sentence that adds information to a main supporting idea, put a semicolon before it and a comma after it.

Example

COMPLETE SENTENCE   TRANSITIONAL WORD   COMPLETE SENTENCE

James speaks several languages;   for example,   he is fluent in Chinese and Russian.

2. When you use a transition to introduce a new supporting idea, put a period before it and a comma after it.

Example

COMPLETE SENTENCE   TRANSITIONAL WORD   COMPLETE SENTENCE

Allen left work and went to the store.   Afterwards,   he drove home and started dinner.

3. Some transitional words can be used inside the second sentence surrounded with commas; others, especially short transitional words, do not require commas.

Example

                                          TRANSITIONAL   VERB +

COMPLETE SENTENCE   SUBJECT   WORD   VERB + COMPLEMENT

We in this class are from all over the world.   I,   for example,   am from Greece.

COMPLETE SENTENCE   SUBJECT

We in this class are from all over the world.   I will eventually know all my classmates,

but for now   I only know Jaime.

TRANSITIONAL WORD   VERB + COMPLEMENT

Transitions for Chronological Sequence

You can use the transitional words in this section to introduce the main supporting sentences in the body of a paragraph. They tell your reader that you have finished explaining the previous point or step and are going to explain another different point at this time.

First

Use *first* in the first supporting sentence to introduce the first step in a process or sequence of events. Do NOT use *first* in the topic sentence.

Example

It is easy to make lasagna if you follow these steps. **First,** gather the ingredients you will need...

Second

Use *second* for the second step. It is not a good idea to continue numbering the steps after the second one, however, because it will make your paragraph sound like a list. In other words, don't write *third, fourth,* or *fifth.* Instead, use words such as *then, after that, next,* or *and then.*

Example

At first, changing a tire may seem difficult, but if you follow these simple steps, you should have no trouble at all. **First,** make sure that the gear of your car is in "park" position. **Second,** set the emergency brake. After that, remove the jack and the spare tire from the trunk of your car, and...

Afterwards, (after)

Afterwards can cause some problems in writing.

Afterwards means "then" or "after that." It is frequently confused with *after,* but be careful, because the two words do not mean the same. *After* is a subordinator punctuated like *because,* and it tells the first action in a sentence; *afterwards* is a transitional word and needs punctuation before and after it. It tells the last action in the sentence.

Examples

We went to the baseball game; **afterwards,** we all went out to dinner. **(This means the same as, "After** we went to the baseball game, we went out to dinner.")

Eventually

Use *eventually* to express "after a period of time."

Examples

Eventually, he understood the idea, but it took several hours of study.

He **eventually** understood the idea, but it took several hours of study.

Finally, all in all, in short, to sum up

The transitional word *finally* is not used to introduce the conclusion of a paragraph. *Finally* is used to introduce the main supporting sentence of the body. To introduce the conclusion, use words such as *in conclusion,* or *all in all.* If the conclusion includes a summary, which happens in longer essays and compositions, you may use the words *in short* and *to sum up.*

(This is the *end* of a paragraph.)

...After Hank was arrested by the police, he confessed to the crime and went to prison. Finally, the family of the victim could rest easily and continue with their lives. **All in all,** we can conclude that even though the justice system is slow, sometimes it is efficient.

● Transitions for Additional Information

In addition, also, furthermore

In addition, also, and *furthermore* are used to show additional information. When you use these transitional words, the information in the second sentence must be closely related to the information in the first sentence. *In addition* and *furthermore* are punctuated like other transitional words, but *also* is different. When *also* is written inside the sentence, it doesn't need commas around it.

Examples

The walls in this room are dark; **in addition,** the carpet and ceiling are somber.

The chalkboard is clean. **Furthermore,** the carpet and ceiling are spotless.

The chalkboard is clean. The carpet and ceiling, **in addition,** are stained.

This room is dark; **also,** the carpet and ceiling are somber.

This room is dark. **Also,** the carpet and ceiling are somber.

The exception:

This room is dark. The carpet and ceiling are **also** somber.

(NO COMMAS)

This room is dark. The carpet and ceiling **also** look somber.

(NO COMMAS)

● Transitions for Illustration

For example, for instance

The phrases *for example* and *for instance* introduce an example. (See also pages 36–38.)

Examples

A good friend has several wonderful qualities; **for example,** a good friend is honest, supportive, helpful, and understanding.

I have many friends who study computer technology. My roommate, John Wilson, **for instance,** studies computer programming with me.

Exercise A2.14   Use the following words in complete and original sentences.

1. in addition _____

_____

2. for instance _____

_____

3. in short _____

_____

4. eventually _____

_____

5. afterwards _____

_____

Exercise A2.15   Fill in the blanks with the most appropriate transitional word or expression. Add correct punctuation in the short blanks.

1. Apartheid is an Afrikaans word that refers to the system of racial segregation and white superiority that began in 1948 in South Africa, and it was extremely unfair to all nonwhites (1) __ _____ blacks, who comprised 75% of all South Africans, were put on bantustans, or small reservations, where the land was so poor that it could not support the population (2) __ _____ Blacks were forbidden to own land, vote, travel, or work without special permits (3) __ _____ interracial sex, marriage, and association were (4) _____ against the law. (5) _____ in 1989,

the new government in South Africa relaxed the apartheid desegregation of some public facilities. Although times are still difficult for blacks in South Africa, some positive changes are (6) _____ being made.

2. This seems to be an especially bad year for severe weather (1) __

_____ it is only July (2) __ yet there are already three tropical depressions in the Atlantic ocean. Usually, the hurricane season comes in August. This is unusual weather.

Exercise A2.16 Use transitional words and expressions and correct punctuation to complete this paragraph. The short blanks are for punctuation. Use periods, semicolons, or commas.

Ruth knew that she had a test today, but she did everything wrong last night to prepare for the exam (1) __ _____ __ she didn't study the correct chapters or review her class notes (2) __ _____ __ she went to bed quite late, did not sleep well, and woke up late for class this morning. Before she went to class, she didn't eat breakfast (3) __ _____ __ she will probably not get a very good grade on her test.

Exercise A2.17 Combine these sentences using coordinating conjunctions, subordinating conjunctions, or transitional words. You may eliminate repeated words.

Example

Niamey is the capital of Niger in West Africa.
Niamey is the center of culture in West Africa.

Niamey is the capital of Niger and the center of culture in West Africa.
_____

1. Baghdad, Iraq, is located where the Tigris and Euphrates rivers are closest.
The rivers flood from time to time.
The city has been hurt by floods several times in the past.

_____

_____

2. Niamey is the capital of Niger in West Africa.
   Niamey is the center of culture in West Africa.

   _____

   _____

3. The land around Niamey is arid.
   Niamey is located on the Niger river.
   Niamey benefits from the water in the Niger.
   Niamey is not arid.

   _____

   _____

   _____

4. Alexandria, Egypt, is not a young city.
   Alexandria, Egypt, is not an agricultural city.

   _____

   _____

5. Alexandria's beaches are popular for many reasons.
   Alexandria's beaches have miles of beautiful white sand.
   Alexandria's beaches have seaside gardens.
   Alexandria has famous resorts.

   _____

   _____

   _____

6. Antananariveo, Madagascar, used to be called Tananarive.
   The name changed in 1794.
   It was captured by Imerina kings in 1794.

   _____

   _____

   _____

Irregular Verbs[1]

Base Form	Past Tense	Past Participle
awake	awoke	awoken
be	was, were	been
beat	beat	beaten
become	became	become
begin	began	begun
bend	bent	bent
bite	bit	bitten
bleed	bled	bled
blow	blew	blown
break	broke	broken
bring	brought	brought
build	built	built
buy	bought	bought
catch	caught	caught
choose	chose	chosen
come	came	come
cost	cost	cost
cut	cut	cut
dig	dug	dug
do	did	done
draw	drew	drawn

---

1 This is not a complete listing of irregular verbs, but they are some of the most frequently used. Check your dictionary for other verbs.

Base Form	Past Tense	Past Participle
drink	drank	drunk
drive	drove	driven
eat	ate	eaten
fall	fell	fallen
feed	fed	fed
feel	felt	felt
fight	fought	fought
find	found	found
fit	fit	fit
fly	flew	flown
forget	forgot	forgotten
forgive	forgave	forgiven
freeze	froze	frozen
get	got	gotten (got)
give	gave	given
go	went	gone
grow	grew	grown
hang	hung	hung
have	had	had
hear	heard	heard
hide	hid	hidden
hit	hit	hit
hold	held	held
hurt	hurt	hurt
keep	kept	kept
know	knew	known
lay	laid	laid
lead	led	led
leave	left	left
let	let	let
lie	lay	lain
light	lit (lighted)	lit (lighted)

Base Form	Past Tense	Past Participle
lose	lost	lost
make	made	made
mean	meant	meant
meet	met	met
pay	paid	paid
put	put	put
quit	quit	quit
read	read	read
ride	rode	ridden
ring	rang	rung
rise	rose	risen
run	ran	run
say	said	said
see	saw	seen
sell	sold	sold
send	sent	sent
set	set	set
shake	shook	shaken
shoot	shot	shot
shut	shut	shut
sing	sang	sung
sit	sat	sat
sleep	slept	slept
slide	slid	slid
speak	spoke	spoken
spend	spent	spent
spread	spread	spread
stand	stood	stood
steal	stole	stolen
stick	stuck	stuck
strike	struck	struck
swear	swore	sworn

Base Form	Past Tense	Past Participle
sweep	swept	swept
swim	swam	swum
take	took	taken
teach	taught	taught
tear	tore	torn
tell	told	told
think	thought	thought
throw	threw	thrown
understand	understood	understood
upset	upset	upset
wake	woke	waked (woken)
wear	wore	worn
weave	wove	woven
win	won	won
withdraw	withdrew	withdrawn
write	wrote	written